Missiology with Power

Missiology with Power

A Missing Dimension
in Intercultural Ministry

CHARLES H. KRAFT

Foreword by Craig S. Keener
Introduction by John Jay Travis

WIPF & STOCK · Eugene, Oregon

MISSIOLOGY WITH POWER
A Missing Dimension in Intercultural Ministry

Copyright © 2024 Charles H. Kraft. All rights reserved. Except for brief quotations in critical publications or reviews, no part of this book may be reproduced in any manner without prior written permission from the publisher. Write: Permissions, Wipf and Stock Publishers, 199 W. 8th Ave., Suite 3, Eugene, OR 97401.

Wipf & Stock
An Imprint of Wipf and Stock Publishers
199 W. 8th Ave., Suite 3
Eugene, OR 97401

www.wipfandstock.com

PAPERBACK ISBN: 979-8-3852-2427-2
HARDCOVER ISBN: 979-8-3852-2428-9
EBOOK ISBN: 979-8-3852-2429-6

VERSION NUMBER 12/30/24

Unless otherwise indicated, Scripture quotations are from the Good News Translation® (Today's English Version, 2nd ed.). Copyright © 1992 American Bible Society. All rights reserved.

CONTENTS

Foreword by Craig S. Keener | vii

Introduction by John Jay Travis | xi

SECTION ONE: BACKGROUND

Chapter 1   Three-Dimensional Missiology | 3

Chapter 2   The Spiritual-Power-Oriented World | 10

Chapter 3   Missiology with Power | 12

Chapter 4   Missiology without Power | 15

Chapter 5   The Biblical Validity | 18

Chapter 6   Satan, the Counterfeit Contextualizer | 22

SECTION TWO: BASIC CONCEPTS

Chapter 7   Forms, Meanings, and Empowerment | 29

Chapter 8   Cultural Constants in the Relationship Between Spirit and Human Worlds | 33

Chapter 9   Animism: Satan's Counterfeit | 37

Chapter 10 Animism Does Not Simply Go Away | 41

Chapter 11 Spiritual Power in Balance | 44

Chapter 12 Two Levels of Conflict | 47

Contents

SECTION THREE: SPECIFIC ISSUES

Chapter 13   Demonization | 55

Chapter 14   Dealing with Inherited Family or Occult Spirits and Generational Spiritual Inheritance | 59

Chapter 15   Gods, Idols, and Divination | 62

Chapter 16   Ancestors and Reincarnation | 65

Chapter 17   Shrines and Dedicated Places | 69

Chapter 18   Blessing, Cursing, and Soul Ties | 71

SECTION FOUR: RECOMMENDED ACTIONS

Chapter 19   What to Do about Forbidden Customs | 75

Chapter 20   Developing Functional Substitutes | 79

Chapter 21   Direct Bridging from Power to Power | 84

Chapter 22   Key Spiritual Dynamics in Intercultural Ministry | 87

Bibliography | 91

Books on Spiritual Power by Charles H. Kraft | 95

FOREWORD

Craig Keener, PhD

JESUS CALLED DISCIPLES TO be with him, to be sent to preach, and to have authority to cast out demons (Mark 3:15). Jesus called his followers to be witnesses, empowered by the Spirit (Acts 1:8), in a two-volume work where "power" is most often expressed in healing and deliverance from demons (Luke 4:36; 5:17; 6:19; 8:46; 9:1; Acts 3:12; 4:7; 6:8; 10:38). Of course, Jesus was speaking to his immediate disciples, but the mission to the ends of the earth (Acts 1:8) continues today, as does the power he granted his first disciples (Acts 2:38–39). That power is not expressed identically in each individual (as Paul notes regarding spiritual gifts), but together the church as a whole must carry on this mission (cf. Matt 28:18–20; John 14:12).

When I was in seminary, I read Charles Kraft's *Christianity in Culture*, an important and influential work on missiology. Although I was taking missions classes, the importance of cultural context and contextualization proved no less crucial in my classes on biblical exegesis. I also learned about power encounters and people movements, and some of what the Western church could learn from global Christianity. Kraft's recognition of not only material but also spiritual realities stands in the historic tradition of the church and the lived reality of the majority of the world's cultures. In the West it seems too easy to embrace an appearance of godliness while denying God's transforming and delivering power.

Although not a missiologist, I also learned some lessons the hard way. My wife, who is Congolese, holds a PhD from a French university, but her ordinary life in Congo exposed her to people who regularly engaged in malevolent spiritual practices that I had barely heard of. Heard of, that is, except in Scripture, in passages that I had unconsciously glided over because they were so far from my cognitive world.

Christians differ among ourselves on details. Many of us cannot endorse all "spiritual warfare" practices around the world; many will not necessarily endorse all those in this book. But those of us devoted to the message of Scripture can hardly deny the reality of spiritual warfare, much less the reality of malevolent spiritual powers. Rather than demeaning as primitive the New Testament worldview about demons—a worldview shared by Jesus, his apostles, and the church through most of history—loyalty to Scripture demands that we question Western reductionist materialism. While materialists have become skilled at explaining the material world, for which we can be grateful, pure materialism's reductionist presuppositions render it blind to spiritual causes. Indeed, experiences like those attributed in the Gospels to severe demonization are reported in a majority of the world's cultures, usually indigenously attributed to spirit activity, even though Western observers often explain them in different ways.[1]

The Bible claims that other spiritual powers are demons (1 Cor 10:20) and warns against workers of signs in the name of false gods (Exod 7:11, 22; 8:7, 18; Deut 13:1–2). It speaks of false prophets with signs and wonders (Matt 24:24; Mark 13:22; Acts 8:9–11; 13:6–10; 19:13–14; 2 Thess 2:8–9; Rev 13:14). Why in the world would we acknowledge the danger of these hostile powers yet insist on stripping Christians of access to God's infinitely greater power to combat these powers? How we do the latter is a legitimate matter of discussion, but neglecting biblical teaching

---

1. See the survey in Keener, *Miracles: Credibility*, 2:788–856; Vaughan, *Phenomenal Phenomena*.

and our fellow believers' accounts of encounters seems hardly an option, especially as many non-Christians even in the West resort increasingly to spiritual power apart from the name of Jesus.

Healings and exorcisms accompanied the early twentieth-century Korean revival, much to the dismay of some of the Western missionaries working there. When the missionaries conducted a study, however, they recognized that genuine miracles and deliverances had taken place. The local Korean Christians thus converted the Western missionaries to a more wholistic approach to God's work in the world. In an influential article, missionary anthropologist Paul Hiebert noted that Indian Christians filled a lacuna in his training. He knew about God and people but lacked a category for preternatural forces until forced to confront them in an Indian context.[2]

Shortly after a trip to Congo, when it became clear to some people known for cursing the family that we were supporting them, I went through a severe spiritual attack on one day, then another on the next. On the third day, my wife and I went out for a walk and stopped under a tree to decide which way to go. No sooner had we stepped out from under the tree than it split at the bottom and came crashing down directly where we had been standing. Although three stories tall, it had wide, full branches from the bottom up and would have crushed us. Médine's brother in Congo, a university chemistry professor, was praying with someone who knew no details of what had occurred. That sister described by the Spirit what happened to me the first and second day and then said she saw a spirit going into a tree to twist it around and asked what that was about.

I knew that was my experience, but I lacked an adequate spiritual explanation for it because I was convinced that, while demons could afflict individuals, they could not do things like knock down trees. I lived in the tension between my experience and my theology until one day, reading the first chapter of Job in Hebrew, I realized that Satan arranged a wind to kill Job's children by knocking down their house (Job 1:19). Although I had read

---

2. Hiebert, "Flaw of the Excluded Middle," 35–47.

Foreword

the passage countless times, I had never allowed it to inform my theology, because my cultural blinders limited what I would see.

Charles Kraft's contribution invites us to look past our cultural blinders and consider how things look from cultures other than our own—cultures sometimes closer to the biblical worldview than is our own.

INTRODUCTION

John Jay Travis, PhD

OVER HIS LONG CAREER of seminary and university teaching, Dr. Charles "Chuck" Kraft has authored more than thirty-five books on topics as varied as linguistics, intercultural communication, anthropology, contextualization, missiology, spiritual power, and healing prayer. This present volume, *Missiology with Power: A Missing Dimension in Intercultural Ministry*, integrates two fields about which Kraft is eminently qualified to write: missiology and spiritual power.

Kraft is a pioneer in the field of missiology[1] and a scholar-practitioner in the area of spiritual power. Over the years he trained and help launch many students into power ministries including my wife and me.[2] As used in this book, spiritual power (or simply "power"/power ministries) is used to refer to miraculous works of God such as physical healing, inner healing, deliverance, signs and wonders, dreams and visions, and other such miracles. Not only

---

1. Kraft's most well-known missiological text is *Christianity in Culture*.

2. My wife and I studied under Kraft in the year 2000, taking his courses on power ministries. I eventually pursued a PhD at Fuller doing a dissertation on the topic of inner healing and deliverance prayer in Muslim contexts. Since Kraft's retirement, I have taught two courses at Fuller that Kraft formerly taught: MO506, "Healing Prayer in Intercultural Ministry," and MO507, "Power Encounter."

Introduction

has Kraft given scholarly attention to spiritual power and power ministries, he has also, by his own estimates, prayed with over five thousand people for inner healing (or what Kraft often calls "deep-level healing"). As a tribute to Kraft, his colleague at Fuller Seminary the late Peter Wagner stated: "No one has made a greater contribution toward introducing the dimension of spiritual power to the discipline of missiology than Chuck Kraft."[3]

Around the year 2004, at a conference put on by the mission agency Frontiers, Kraft and his prayer team that we were part of prayed for about one hundred missionaries, or *cross-cultural field workers*,[4] who were working in Muslim contexts. These field workers came to the conference from many different parts of Asia, Africa, and the Middle East. Many had worked in hard and discouraging places for a long time and came to the conference hoping to gain fresh perspective as well as a much-needed touch from the Lord. Many of those one hundred workers who received inner-healing prayer were greatly encouraged! They took this model of prayer back to the places where they worked and started praying for teammates and Muslim friends alike. Today this kind of prayer is widely used in Frontiers and many field teams have integrated it into their missiological practice.[5] In addition, besides answering prayers for healing and deliverance, God is also giving dreams and visions of Jesus to many Muslims.

---

3. Wagner, "Missiology and Spiritual Power," 91.

4. Cross-cultural field worker or intercultural field worker is a term commonly used in place of missionary. In much of the world today, missionary visas are not available or permitted. Christians working in cross-cultural or intercultural settings are bivocational, working in some tentmaking capacity. In addition, in some parts of the world, the term missionary carries unhelpful cultural baggage. For purposes of this book, whether using the term missionary, cross-cultural worker, or intercultural worker, Kraft is referring to a follower of Jesus who is crossing some form of social, cultural, or religious barrier to share the good news of Jesus with others in particular contexts or communities.

5. For an explanation of inner-healing or "deep-healing" prayer, see the list of Kraft's books at the end of this volume. In addition, see Ann Muller's *Two Hands: A Guide to Inner Healing Prayer*. The model of prayer Muller presents has been widely used in numerous cultural and socio-religious contexts.

Introduction

This kind of news makes Chuck Kraft's heart glad! He longs to see field workers learn how to pray for blessing, physical healing, inner healing, and deliverance in cross-cultural ministry. He longs to hear of God going ahead of field workers, giving dreams and visions to those who do not yet follow Jesus. He also hopes for robust discussions among workers about the contextualizing of power ministries. In *Missiology with Power* he articulates this longing and his hope for the book:

> Where today are the discussions concerning biblically legitimate and culturally appropriate approaches to areas of life such as spiritual conflict prayer, deliverance from demons, healing, blessing and cursing, dedications, visions, dreams, concepts of the territoriality of spirits, angels, demons, and the like? Shouldn't we be discussing the contextualizing of a biblical approach to spiritual conflict? What are the scriptural principles applicable to every cultural situation, and what are the cultural variables in this important area? These important issues need to be addressed. I pray that this book will be a helpful step in the right direction (14).

Chuck Kraft, however, wasn't always passionate about this, nor was he an expert in healing prayer and spiritual conflict. Referring to when he served as a missionary in West Africa in the 1950s, he states that he was unprepared theoretically and practically to deal with the spiritual questions being asked by the village leaders with whom he worked. Many had more interest in what the Bible taught on evil spirits and curses than they did on many of the finer theological points Kraft was trained to teach.

After returning to the United States, Kraft became a university and seminary professor, most notably at Fuller Seminary. While at Fuller in the early 1980s, Kraft determined that ministries involving spiritual power, such as healing and deliverance, were crucial, yet often missing in both missiological practice and the Christian life in general. Once he realized the importance of this "missing dimension" he applied himself through prayer, study, and participation to learn all he could about these types of ministries.

Introduction

He was soon teaching courses on spiritual power at Fuller and continued to do so until his retirement in 2007.

Kraft does not want to see cross-cultural field workers today uninformed and ill-equipped as he was during his service as a missionary. Kraft's passion is that those called to bring the message of Jesus to others today would not only have a good grasp of Scripture and culture, but also learn how to engage in power ministries, both in the proclamation of the gospel and in the process of discipleship. During this time of discipleship new followers of Jesus will turn away from harmful spiritual powers and practices, developing biblically sound, "functional substitutes" to replace any power rituals they had formerly relied on before following Jesus (see chapter 20). If these biblically sound substitutes are not found, Kraft fears the spiritual condition he calls "dual allegiance" may be the result: following Jesus intellectually and outwardly but secretly returning to former unholy sources of power for healing and the like in times of need.

This book, however, is not a guide or handbook on specifically how to engage in power ministries.[6] Rather, the greater concern of this book is to lay out a foundation of why the study of missiology is incomplete without incorporating the matter of power ministries and the development of biblically sound, functional substitutes. Before saying more about the book, I will share some relevant thoughts on missiology and spiritual power in general.

Expressed succinctly, missiology is the study of how the good news of Jesus is communicated in cultural and religious contexts where few, if any, yet follow Christ. A hope of missiology is not only to help individuals receive Jesus as Lord but rather entire communities as well. In order for this hope to be realized, missiologists seek to share the good news of Jesus in ways that are understandable, relevant, and viable.

---

6. For sources on how to engage in this type of ministry, see books by Kraft at the end of the book. Also see MacNutt, *Healing*; Wimber, *Power Evangelism*; Wimber, *Power Healing*.

Introduction

Being understandable means that the truths of the Bible are presented in words, concepts, and communication styles that make sense to people in different cultural and religious contexts.

Being relevant means that the good news addresses felt needs and real-life issues in the lives of the people involved. Jesus is our prime example of this: whether dealing with the blind, the leper, the outcast, the confused, the demonized, or demoralized, Jesus sought first to show that the message and power of the kingdom of God was there through him, and that he was willing and able to heal and touch people at the place of their deepest pain and need.

Being viable is a related, yet distinct, third step. Once people understand the message of Jesus and see its relevancy, being viable means that this new life in Christ is experienced as a doable, real, actual life-choice for them and their community. While it is ultimately God who draws people to follow Jesus (John 6:44), it is also true that cultural and socio-religious factors can hinder the process.[7] A key dynamic of missiology, therefore, is making sure that no unnecessary requirements or cultural trappings are encumbering the gospel message, such that it seems unattainable or foreign, not a real, viable life-option for the average person. It follows, as well, that being viable implies that different contexts (e.g., tribal peoples, Buddhists, Hindus, Muslims, Shintos, etc.) will develop different forms or expressions of following Jesus.[8] Yet apart from issues such as culture, language, and socio-religious background, there is another dynamic in which the concept of viability must be understood. This other dynamic is what might be called "spiritual" viability.

Virtually all peoples—adherents of the world's major religious traditions, devotees of smaller folk religions/tribal faiths, nominal Christians, even atheists—have a myriad of beliefs and practices that they have turned to all of their lives to help them

---

7. Acts 15 records how Paul, Barnabas, and others realized that the situation of circumcision was an enormous social, cultural, and socio-religious barrier to the spread of the gospel.

8. See Bishop, *Boundless*. This fascinating study shows a wide variety of the types of expressions of following Jesus found today in certain groups including Buddhists, Muslims, and several others.

Introduction

in times of need.⁹ These beliefs and practices often invoke "spiritual power" or powers that involve telling the future, numerology, divination, healing from disease, freedom from evil spirits, insuring good fortune, and so forth. They would feel lost and powerless without these practices and powers being available to them once they decide to follow Jesus. This is likely what was behind the questions African Christians put to Kraft in the 1950s, and similar to questions I have heard many times working in Southeast Asia.

Dudley Woodberry, another colleague of Kraft's at Fuller, provides us with a very helpful six-fold rubric for understanding how most of the world sees spiritual power(s): power people, power objects, power places, power rituals, power times, and power beings.[10]

1. Power people—traditional healers, shamans, diviners, exorcists

2. Power objects—charms, amulets, house idols, magic scrolls, "evil eye"

3. Power places—shrines, holy ground, certain caves, trees, and bodies of water

4. Power rituals—dedications to spirits or gods, incantations, numerology, cursing, blessing

5. Power times—auspicious times of day, days of the week, seasons, or holy days

6. Power beings—spirits, *jinn*, local deities, angels

Throughout *Missiology with Power*, Kraft gives examples of these types of powers from a variety of cultural contexts.

The book has twenty-two chapters and is divided into four sections. In the first section, Kraft shares his own journey as a missionary in Africa, a time (as alluded to above) when he realized he had a "missiology without power." He also shares in the first

---

9. See Hiebert et al., *Understanding Folk Religion* for an excellent study on folk religions and animism.

10. See Woodberry, "Relevance of Power Ministries," 313–31.

section the idea of the three dimensions of our Christ-centered witness: the power dimension, the truth dimension, and the relationship or allegiance-with-God dimension, and how these three dimensions are all needed in outreach and discipleship.

In the second section, Kraft unpacks how certain practices and beliefs common in animism, folk religion, and any religious expression (including nominal Christianity) that seeks sources of spiritual power outside of the one true God can open the door for satanic influence. He also, in this section (chapter 12), shares his view on what many call "territorial" spirits. Kraft and others also refer to these types of spirits as "cosmic-level" spirits.[11]

By contrast with cosmic-level spirits discussed in the second section, the third section deals with what Kraft calls "ground-level" spirits, the kind that attach to or attack individuals. He shares how cross-cultural workers need to know how to pray when people have become oppressed by ground-level demonic powers through various forms of magic, shrine and idol worship, dedications to local deities, divination, vows, numerology, amulets, cursing, and other related practices.

In the final section, Kraft addresses what cross-cultural workers can do to be best prepared for spiritual conflict and to know how to use the power and truth of Jesus to set people free from satanic influence in their lives and communities. It is in here he elaborates on the need for Christ-centered, functional substitutes. At the end of the book is a list of publications of Chuck Kraft on the topics of spiritual power.

Recently Kraft asked me if I thought that in current missiological practice, power ministries were more widely understood and embraced than they were, say, in the 1980s and 1990s, a time when many books were beginning to be published on this topic.

I responded that I have seen some shifts in thinking and practices since I first moved and worked overseas in the 1980s. At that time, I think that most evangelical cross-cultural workers at least had room for miracles in their missiology and theology. It seems

---

11. Beilby and Eddy provide excellent discussions on the topic of territorial spirits in their edited work *Four Views of Spiritual Warfare*.

Introduction

as well that if called upon to pray for healing or deliverance—freedom from demonic oppression or bondage—most would. My sense is, however, that most did not see power ministries at that time as a major part of their ministry.

Steadily from that time until the present, however, I have seen prayer for healing becoming increasingly practiced by field workers. Discussions on spiritual conflict are not at all uncommon. In addition, many now combine deliverance prayer with inner-healing prayer, a type of prayer that brings the power and presence of Jesus to people suffering from trauma, rejection, painful memories, damaged emotions, and heart wounds. Many see Jesus as our role model for inner healing based upon numerous biblical narratives.[12] Many workers today are also aware of the importance of a second aspect of inner healing which involves confessing any known transgressions and renouncing any ungodly practices and allegiances.

I went on to say to Kraft, however, that in spite of these encouraging trends, we still have so much to learn. We need to develop better spiritual eyes to see where spiritual bondages may be present in any particular culture or milieu (including our own). We also need to rely on the Spirit and Scripture to develop the best means possible of spiritually helping to set people free.

That is where this book comes in as a great resource. In the pages that follow, Kraft carefully takes the reader on a journey of understanding worldview, the unseen spiritual realm, the importance of power, truth, and allegiance encounters, and how this all works together in cross-cultural ministry. In short, this book is designed to assist intercultural field workers to know how they can

---

12. Examples include the heart-healing and restoration of the guilt-ridden Peter (John 21), the ostracized woman at the well (John 4), the grateful woman who washed the feet of Jesus with her tears (Luke 7), the rescued adulteress (John 8), the blind man emboldened by Jesus (John 9), the unclean hemorrhaging woman (Mark 5), and the tormented wild man freed of Legion (Luke 8). In each of these touching encounters with Jesus (which sometimes involved physical healing and deliverance), we see Jesus, through his loving and powerful actions and words, healing broken hearts and shattered lives, taking away rejection, shame, and sorrow. This is inner healing.

Introduction

best help people "turn from darkness to light and from the power of Satan to God" (Acts 26:18) so that in Jesus, they can fully live out the destiny God has for them.

SECTION ONE

BACKGROUND

Chapter 1

THREE-DIMENSIONAL MISSIOLOGY

I BELIEVE THE MISSIOLOGY that many of us learned and used cross-culturally was in some ways deficient. We were strong on the relational aspects of following Jesus but weak in the area of spiritual power.

There were at least three crucial dimensions to being a disciple of Jesus that Jesus practiced and taught. The first and most important of these dimensions is what I call the "allegiance-leading-to-relationship dimension." Jesus put relationship first when he summarized the Great Commandment, "Love the Lord your God with all your heart, with all your soul, and with all your mind. And you shall love your neighbor as yourself" (Matt 22:37–39).

Jesus also taught truth. But as he taught truth, he appealed for humans to get into a relationship with him—to pledge allegiance to him and to grow in that intimate relationship. He said things like, "If I be lifted up, I will draw all people to myself" (John 12:32) and, "Come to me all you who are tired from carrying heavy loads" (Matt 11:28). This allegiance or relationship dimension is the most important of the three. The other two support it.

Truth or knowledge, then, is an important supporting dimension. We need a certain amount of knowledge of the truth to

SECTION ONE: BACKGROUND

be able to respond to God. So Jesus taught truth, enabling people to gain enough understanding for them to turn to God and to grow in their relationship with God. Knowledge is important, even though it is to function in a supporting role. We need to know our faith both cognitively and experientially. Jesus said, "You will know [by experience] the Truth and the [experienced] Truth will set you free" (John 8:32).

Knowing truth is not the same as being in a relationship with Jesus. One gains truth at least partially by learning information. This aspect of truth tends to get overemphasized in some streams of evangelical Christianity. But one also experiences truth by putting truth into practice in everyday life. There is observational truth, cognitive truth, and experiential truth. The kind of truth in focus in Scripture is largely the latter—experiential truth. We need to know certain things to support and grow in our relationship with God. Relationship and truth are two of the crucial dimensions.

The third dimension often gets neglected. This is another supporting dimension—"spiritual power leading to freedom"— the freedom people need to respond to the truth they have heard and grow into the saving and freeing relationship we are promised. We are promised that we will become new creatures if we are "in Christ" (2 Cor 5:17). But for many, this promise is not completely fulfilled when they come to Christ. They are saved but not fully free.

According to Jesus, people—even his followers—can live in a type of spiritual captivity. He came to "set captives free" (Luke 4:18–19). But the enemy of our souls, the one Scripture calls Satan or "the Accuser," has been very effective in keeping people (both those who follow Christ and those who don't yet follow him) from the freedom that Jesus came to bring. This hindrance is spiritual and people need spiritual power to get it out of the way. It is this dimension that is usually missing in our missiological training and practice.

The three dimensions can be pictured as follows:

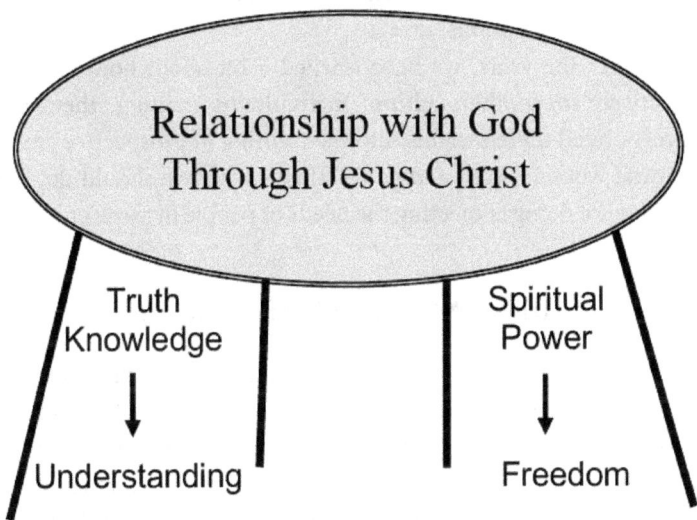

As soon as Jesus received the Holy Spirit and joined John the Baptist's faith-renewal movement, he began using his power to show his love (part of the relational dimension). The people of his day, like those of our day, sought freedom, health, and blessing. And Jesus met them where they were. He was receptor-oriented and worked in ways that were meaningful to his audience. When they came to him in faith with needs for spiritual power, he met their needs in ways they understood and valued.

Though he also taught much truth, Jesus never settled for the intellectualism that has taken over many streams of Christianity today. Jesus was out ministering to people, using the tools God the Father had given him—among them the authority to heal. People came to him who were not free physically, emotionally, or spiritually. And he healed them as an act of his love for them.

Missionaries/cross-cultural workers need special training to function effectively in a cultural world other than the one in which they grew up. Typically, they have learned to function well in their own culture. But now they are being asked to enter the world of a people for whom a different set of actions and reactions is normal. They are being asked to work cross-culturally—to learn another

SECTION ONE: BACKGROUND

way of looking at the world and to work according to another set of cultural assumptions.

Over the years, we have learned a bit about how to work effectively in another culture. Intercultural training, then, has incorporated these insights into the training of prospective cross-cultural workers. Well and good. This is what we should do. But how are we doing at meeting the needs of people in those cultures?

DEALING WITH THE SPIRITS

"What is your biggest problem?" I asked. I was an American missionary in rural Nigeria working with a group of five or six church leaders in a new area for ministry. I had learned the trade language, Hausa, and we were chatting informally as we regularly did, discussing matters pertaining to the introduction of the Good News into the tribal area that these leaders represented.

We regularly discussed our strategies for spreading the gospel on the mountains and in the valleys populated by those who spoke their language. We also discussed theological concepts in our informal times and in our more formal Bible-study sessions. I went with them on evangelistic trips. I watched as they interviewed new followers of Jesus in their home language, Kamwe, which I hadn't learned yet. Those who wanted to join the fellowship were baptized. We discussed the sermons these leaders preached, the moral and spiritual problems they faced with new believers, and anything else that came up concerning their life and ministry. Mine was a steep learning curve as we often got into discussions of their customs.

But when it came to the question of their biggest problem, I wasn't prepared for their answer. They all agreed that the question was, "What do we do about evil spirits?"

They had asked me earlier if I believed in evil spirits. I really didn't know since I was unaware of any personal interaction with them. So I asked, "Have you had some experience with them?" When they then told me some of their experiences with spirits, I said something like, "I trust you and your experiences, so I believe in them." But I'm not sure that was an entirely accurate statement.

MY TRAINING

I was trained well to serve as a missionary. Unlike most of my colleagues, I had studied anthropology to enable me to learn, respect, and understand different cultures, as well as to work within them toward contextualized forms of following Jesus. And I was trained in linguistics to help me learn the languages of my host country. Further, I did a three-year seminary program to get a firm theological foundation. Then I spent a full year beyond seminary studying what we now call missiology and became a PhD candidate in anthropology. I was, I thought, well prepared to work in a pioneering situation, with an animistic,[1] pre-literate people. My aim was to learn their language, reduce it to writing, and work toward a Bible translation.

And much went well. After learning the trade language, Hausa, I was working on learning the home language of the Kamwe people, whom we were assigned to work with. I established good rapport with the few Christian leaders in the area. The Christian community was growing nicely under their leadership, with little missionary leadership. We saw ourselves as their helpers.

But, in discussions with these leaders, I found myself in a very embarrassing position. How could I help these leaders to deal with their number-one problem? Well trained as I was, I had never been taught to deal with spiritual power. Oh, I remembered a theology course in seminary with a textbook that had a section at the end on "Satan and Demons." But we never got to that part of the book! The professor ended the course with the suggestion that we read that part on our own.

So, what I took to Nigeria was a form of following Jesus like I had known at home; with hardly any formation around spiritual

---

1. By *animistic* I mean the holding of a worldview that recognizes unseen spirits and forces at work in nature and inanimate objects, and endeavors to directly influence, control, or be involved with them by various means.

SECTION ONE: BACKGROUND

power (e.g., miracles, healings, deliverances), my secularized discipleship was missing the dimension that most concerned our community.

God blessed the ministry in spite of our inadequacies. The recently planted church that I was to assist experienced gratifying growth. Many people came to the Lord. We were able to start churches in new areas and watch them run almost totally under the care of capable Nigerian brothers and sisters. I had learned that if a church is to be theirs, rather than foreign, it needs to be so from the start. So, from the start, I took the position of advisor and coach in this young church, rather than director. I refused to preach. I refused any official position in the church structure. So it was the Kamwe church from the beginning.

However, many believers began having what I call "dual allegiance." They were committed to Christ and rejoicing in their relationship with him. But neither they nor their leaders had learned that followers of Jesus are to be involved in the kind of spiritual-power encounters that Jesus was in, such as physical healing, inner healing, and deliverance.

They frequently felt the need for spiritual power in their lives, but as sincere as they were in their devotion to Christ, they seldom went to Jesus expectantly for power. When their children got sick, they went both to the shaman and to the mission dispensary. When their crops did not bear or their animals got sick, they went both to the shaman and to the mission agriculturist. When they needed protection, they went to the shaman for advice and to the missionaries who showed them how to build better fences.

In short, they got spiritual solutions from the shamans and secular answers from the missionaries. When they needed spiritual power, they turned to their shamans, for there was little focus on spiritual power in the church.

I have been greatly ashamed that I did not know how to help my Nigerian students with their attempts to deal with the spirit world. They deserved better from me in dealing with spiritual dynamics. And I deserved better from my training.

Traditional Pentecostal missionaries have done a better job than evangelicals in the area of spiritual power. But they, too, have tended to produce a secularized faith like that in their home countries—strong on love but weak on power.

I am writing this book to assist in enlightening cross-cultural workers and those who partner with them concerning what I believe is an oft-ignored dimension of training and ministry. I have been learning a lot over the last several years in this area, in both practice and theory. I have made a commitment that I will not let cross-cultural workers who come my way for training and insight go away as ignorant as I once was in this power dimension.

The following chapters point out several power issues that those in cross-cultural ministry need to address in addition to the very important cultural issues they will face in the field.

Chapter 2

THE SPIRITUAL-POWER-ORIENTED WORLD

Fast-forwarding several years after my experience in Nigeria, I became a missiologist, studying the peoples of the world in their cultures and seeking to help cross-cultural workers share Christ with them. My job has been to relate with people in their cultures and to assist cross-cultural workers to work within the contexts of the world's peoples to communicate Christ and see God's kingdom advance as effectively as possible.

As I learned from people in their cultures and asked questions concerning how best to share the good news of Jesus, it became apparent that what often motivated majority-world people had to do with the invisible spirit world around them.

I learned that outside the West, many people are very aware that a world of spirits exists that can interfere with their daily lives. From earliest childhood they learn that they have to keep these spirits happy or the spirits may cause trouble for them. In many parts of the world, people build shrines as places to perform rituals to gain blessings or keep the spirits at bay.

On one of my trips to Japan, a Japanese student of mine and I stood outside a shrine and surveyed people concerning the reasons they went to that shrine. Some were anxious to get help to

The Spiritual-Power-Oriented World

pass university examinations. Others were concerned that they be able to have children. Some were appealing to the spirits for healing. And I noticed that there were advertisements on the trains that guided people to certain shrines for certain problems. These observations made me wonder if there could be Christian or Jesus-centered "shrines."

Then in Thailand, I noticed that many of the buildings, including the hotel where we stayed, had "spirit houses," which were miniature houses perched on poles outside of the main house. Each morning, then, there would be food placed on a platform in front of these miniature houses. I learned that the object was to get the spirits "to live in their own houses" so that they would not bother whatever went on in the larger building.

Likewise, in Papua New Guinea I saw evidence of sacrifices offered to spirits and talked to missionaries who told me that even the local Christians often offered sacrifices to protect themselves from evil spirits. Such experiences helped me to remember some of the things I had seen in Nigeria that I didn't understand. On many occasions as we walked along the paths, we would see evidence that a chicken had been sacrificed, usually where paths crossed. When I asked, I found that such sacrifices were intended to confuse spirits so they would not follow people home. And I heard stories of diviners who used marks made by crabs in the sand to reveal the future.

But I didn't know what to do about it.

Chapter 3

MISSIOLOGY WITH POWER

It wasn't until 1982, while teaching at Fuller, that I learned more about what I now refer to as "missiology with power." We on the faculty of the Fuller School of World Mission allowed ourselves to be taught on the subject by John Wimber.[1] He taught us through lectures and demonstrations that God's power to heal and deliver from demons is still available today, and that we could and should be using that power in our cross-cultural ministries.[2]

In short, we began to see that the form of following Jesus that we were bringing with us to other cultures was strong in the dimensions of truth and allegiance but weak and uninformed in how

---

1. John Wimber wrote two books in 1986 that describe this theology and practice: *Power Healing* and *Power Evangelism*.

2. Three recent publications emphasize similar themes to those of Wimber. The first is Craig Keener's extremely well-documented book on healing and miracles today, *Miracles Today: The Supernatural Work of God in the Modern World*. His examples of healings come from many cultures. Robby Dawkins's *Do Greater Things: Activating the Kingdom to Heal the Sick and Love the Lost* is a round-the-world journey of healing and miracles taking place in some of the world's most physically dangerous locations. Jon Thompson's *Deliverance: A Journey Toward the Unexpected* deals with the ministry of deliverance in a large church setting in Canada. The connection with Wimber is that these three contemporary books demonstrate convincingly that God still does miracles in our day, similar to what Wimber said to his contemporaries in his day.

Missiology With Power

to deal with the types of spiritual powers I saw people confronting in Japan, Thailand, and Papua New Guinea. This weakness led to a dual-allegiance form of faith, where Christians may attend church quite sincerely on Sunday, but when they need power on Monday, they go to the shaman or other local power practitioner. And this dual allegiance, I contend, is one of the biggest problems worldwide in the church today.

So I would like to encourage the formation of Christ-centered training programs for cross-cultural workers that address not only cultural and theological issues, but also speak to the primary concern of many peoples of the world: spiritual power. This will require that we teach about spiritual power and also that we learn by experience what to do about it. We must work with the topic theoretically and also in practice, similar to what John Wimber did in the courses he taught at Fuller Seminary in the 1980s and which we have continued to teach since then. (Note: in such courses, students are required to do a practicum where they both receive prayer and learn to pray for others.)

These types of training programs are needed because most peoples of the world today participate at some level in spiritual activities that directly and indirectly expose them to evil supernatural powers. Even a casual observation of the world Christian scene leads to the conclusion that a large percentage of the world's Christians are also, in fact, participating in a dual allegiance form of faith. They find in the way of faith that they have been taught little or none of the spiritual power they crave to meet their needs for healing, blessing, guidance, or deliverance from demons. So they continue in their traditional cultural practices of going to shamans, diviners, occult practitioners, temples, shrines, and the like for spiritual power.

This being so, it is strange that we find a relatively limited discussion of spiritual power in the study of missiology, the theory and practice of missions. Western missionaries, development workers, and others who seek to serve cross-culturally have ignored this facet of biblical teaching and ministry. Western worldview blindness has dominated the thinking of cross-cultural workers, though

SECTION ONE: BACKGROUND

they work among people whose thinking and behavior is saturated with a consciousness of the spirit world. And just as that blindness kept many missionaries of the past from ever learning to work adequately with these issues, so it can blind us today as well. We need to give attention to missiology with spiritual power so that we can equip new followers of Jesus in ways that are not only biblically and culturally appropriate but infused with God's power as well.

Where today are the discussions concerning biblically legitimate and culturally appropriate approaches to areas of life such as spiritual conflict prayer, deliverance from demons, healing, blessing and cursing, dedications, visions, dreams, concepts of the territoriality of spirits, angels, demons, and the like? Shouldn't we be discussing the contextualizing of a biblical approach to spiritual conflict? What are the scriptural principles applicable to every cultural situation, and what are the cultural variables in this important area? These important issues need to be addressed. I pray that this book will be a helpful step in the right direction.

Chapter 4

MISSIOLOGY WITHOUT POWER

WHEN I LEFT THE US to work in Nigeria, I was well trained in the areas that Western missionaries generally emphasized—biblical analysis, systematic theology, anthropology, and linguistics. In that sense, my missiology was strong. However, in other dimensions—healing, deliverance, spiritual conflict, etc.—my missiology was uninformed and lacking in power. It was what I call today "missiology without power." I worked well with the Nigerian leaders to develop biblically sound ways of following Jesus that were truly theirs, not merely imports from my own Western culture. But they knew and I knew that there were spiritual dynamics taking place around us that Westerners didn't know how to address.

Some of the local Nigerian Christians learned that they could oppose demonic spiritual powers with the power of Christ. But, as close as I was to them, I did not have the chance to learn from them. So my missiology remained uninformed and lacking in the area of dealing with satanic activity. Again, it was a missiology strong on working with and in the receptors' culture, learning the language and culture, and affirming the right of local Christians to follow Jesus in their own way based on the Bible. However, it was a missiology that was only two dimensional. We were steeped in theological knowledge and firmly committed to biblical truth.

SECTION ONE: BACKGROUND

We also knew we must advocate for a relationship with God, as we strongly felt people's need for that relationship and for its basis of Scriptural truth. Indeed, many of my generation saw truth as the primary concern and relationship with God as a by-product of that truth. That is, we felt that if we taught enough truth, people would come to Christ and grow in their faith.

JESUS GAVE HIS FOLLOWERS THE HOLY SPIRIT

We focused a lot on Acts 1:8: "But when the Holy Spirit comes upon you, you will be filled with power, and you will be witnesses for me in Jerusalem, in all of Judea and Samaria, and to the ends of the earth."

But we ignored the power and the part that the Holy Spirit was to play in our (and his) mission. The disciples were told to wait for the Holy Spirit and his power. Not knowing what this meant, we charged ahead, lacking in power but full of love. Since the love was there, our basic theory was not detrimental, but incomplete. For when it came to power, most of what we had to offer was secular, human power—secular medicine, Sunday lectures (sermons), and secular agriculture. There was prayer, but as far as anyone could tell, the medicine, agriculture, and transmission of information through sermonizing worked just as well with or without prayer. The praying we learned and taught lacked a focus on the power that the Holy Spirit gives to meet the daily spiritual needs that people faced.

In giving his followers the Holy Spirit, Jesus gave them his own authority and power (Luke 9:1). He then promised that when the Holy Spirit comes, he will guide them into all truth (John 16:13). It is the presence of the Holy Spirit that empowers his followers. This gift is given freely to every believer to enable us to do the things he wants us to do.

This is power wrapped in love, a requirement if we are to be truly incarnational in our ministry and training. We need to learn and teach that we have his power, as well as how to use it in ministry to demonstrate God's love. By faith we obtain salvation, and the

Holy Spirit comes to dwell within us. We then are welcomed into a relationship with God and empowered. But we need to learn what to do about this power.

I learned that in the majority of world cultures, people are very aware that a world of spirits exists that can interfere with their daily lives. From earliest childhood, people learn to keep these spirits happy because they may cause trouble. In many parts of the world, people build shrines as places to perform rituals in order to gain blessings or keep the spirits at bay.

I didn't know what to do about this. I was the product of an educational system in which we are taught to focus on "information about" various aspects of life and the world around us. In schools, we received very little practice in "doing" life. We thought about life and a whole lot of less relevant things, nearly always with a focus on knowing rather than experiencing.

Western power concerns tend to be focused on controlling the universe (the physical sciences) and people (the social sciences and politics). We are taught that "knowledge is power" and that we can control our lives through gaining knowledge.

And the church falls right into this trap. Our sermons tend to be history, ethics, or language lectures. We are given lots of advice and knowledge about what we're supposed to do. Since our society doesn't believe in spiritual power, most of our churches don't either. We turn to secular medicine for healing, secular psychology for emotional difficulty, and secular, information-laden schooling for training our spiritual leaders. And some of those who start out training for church leadership discontinue the work either before or soon after they become pastors, since pastoring requires certain skills that were not included in their training.

We say we want to be like Jesus and minister like he did. But the school Jesus founded doesn't look like the schools we establish. Jesus called men and women to "be with him" in apprenticeship, learning by doing what he was doing, not just thinking about what he was doing. And prominent among the things he taught and demonstrated was how to deal with spiritual power—both satanic and Godly forms.

Chapter 5

THE BIBLICAL VALIDITY

THOUGH THE CONCEPT HAS been questioned by some, it has been my perspective and experience that spiritual conflict[1] is an important biblical reality. Many cross-cultural workers have come to the same conclusion based upon their encounters in a variety of cultural milieus.[2] As recorded in Scripture, Jesus treated Satan and demonic spirits as real foes, frequently casting out demons and thus setting people free. He calls Satan "the ruler of this world" (John 14:30). In a similar vein, Paul refers to Satan as "the evil god of this world" who blinds people to God's good news (2 Cor 4:4), and John says, "the whole world is under the rule of the Evil One" (1 John 5:19).

---

1. See Beilby and Eddy, *Understanding Spiritual Warfare*, for excellent articles on spiritual conflict.

2. For examples of cross-cultural workers reporting on spiritual conflict in their ministry contexts and the need for further understanding and equipping for ministry see chapters 9–12 of Wagner and Pennoyer, *Wrestling with Dark Angels*. See also the article on inner healing in cross-cultural contexts by Travis and Travis, "Deep-Level Healing Prayer," in *Paradigm Shifts*. In the same volume, Tormod Engelsviken provides a very helpful discussion on his experiences in Ethiopia and his call for deeper understanding and engagement on the part of Western churches in his article "Spiritual Conflict."

The Biblical Validity

Like most of the world today, biblical peoples saw the world as populated by enemy spirits that could cause trouble if they were not properly dealt with. Unfortunately, through most of its history the people of Israel chose to deal with these spirits as the animistic peoples around them did, rather than as God commanded them to. God constantly warned his people against worshiping the gods (=demons) of the nations around them and they suffered dire consequences when they rebelled. We know that our God is a patient God. He has demonstrated this countless times in his interactions with human beings. But there are areas of life, especially those that involve the counterfeiting of his power-oriented activities, in which he has made it clear that there is to be no compromise.

Note, as one of many examples, what God said to Solomon in 1 Kgs 11 (especially vv. 9–13) concerning the penalty Solomon would have to pay because he rebelled against God by turning to other gods. God was angry with Solomon and the kingdom was taken away from his son because of his idolatry. In Acts 5, Peter asks Ananias why he "let Satan take control" of him (v. 3) that he should lie to the Holy Spirit about the price of the property he had sold. And in 1 Cor 10:20–21, we are warned against eating what has been offered to demons. This warning is then given even more sternly in Rev 2:14 and 20.

Jesus came "to destroy what the Devil had done" (1 John 3:8). He gives his followers "power and authority to drive out all demons and to cure diseases" (Luke 9:1) and to do the works that he himself did while on earth (John 14:12). We can't be either biblical or relevant to most of the peoples of the world without a solid approach to spiritual power.

In all of this, we need to know who we are in Christ and what difference this makes when we assert the authority we have in Christ in the spirit world. Satan knows who we are and is afraid we'll understand our true spiritual identity in Christ.[3] If we find out who we are, we are likely to begin ministering in power and defeating Satan. Among the publications on this subject, one of my favorites is Neil Anderson's *Victory over the Darkness*.

3. Kraft, *Satan Fears*.

SECTION ONE: BACKGROUND

JESUS PREDICTED THAT WE WOULD DO WHAT HE DID

Cross-cultural workers often speak of practicing "incarnational ministry"—doing the ministry according to Jesus' example, as he said we would. He said, "Whoever has faith in me will do the works that I have been doing" (John 14:12, my translation), and "As the Father has sent me, so I send you" (John 20:21).

Jesus had set the pattern for us by saying these things. He also demonstrated what he meant by sending his disciples out to "preach the Kingdom of God and to heal the sick" (Luke 9:2). They were not to evangelize only with words but with healings as well. The disciples got the point and "traveled through all the villages, preaching the good news and healing people everywhere" (Luke 9:6). A similar set of commands was given to a larger group of Jesus' followers (Luke 10:1–8), who came back from their time in the field and reported to Jesus that "even the demons obeyed us when we gave them a command in your name" (Luke 10:17).

If we are to truly follow our Master in ministry, we should start where he started, with the filling of the Holy Spirit (Luke 3:21–22) and receiving of God's power to do God's work. Then, like Jesus, we are to go into ministry, communicating and healing in love and power. Jesus was a man working with the authority of the Holy Spirit. We are to practice incarnational ministry under the same Holy Spirit, with authority, empowerment, and results.

OUR AUTHORITY AND POWER

Satan is very good at protecting himself from what he knows to be a power much greater than his. Satan knows that God has infinitely more power than he has and that Jesus passed this power on to us. His primary strategy, therefore, is to keep God's people ignorant and deceived so that they cannot use God's power against him.

A very important first step in contextualizing spiritual power, therefore, is to help people to know who they are scripturally and how this is to be expressed culturally. Scripturally, we are the children of God, made in his image, and redeemed by Jesus Christ to be joint heirs of God with him (Rom 8:17). This gives us all the power and authority Jesus gave his followers to cast out demons and cure diseases (Luke 9:1), to do the works Jesus himself did (John 14:12), to be in this world what Jesus was (John 20:21), and to crush the enemy under our feet (Rom 16:20). Scripturally, then, we need to follow Jesus' example, always using his power to show his love.

Christ's followers worldwide are accountable to God to resist traditional cultural models for the exercise of power. Instead, we need to discover or create relevant models of power with local believers and leaders that are consonant with Scripture. Appropriate ways of expressing and exercising power in love within various cultural contexts may look quite different from each other. Many Western missionaries set a poor example of scriptural contextualization in this area, often showing captivity to home cultural models rather than working out scripturally appropriate contextualizations of traditional customs.

Western exercise of spiritual power tends to replace scriptural expressions with secular practices. For healing, we use medicine and hospitals, with or without prayer. For food production and other areas of life, we follow Western patterns, usually without prayer. In a sense, we have secularized the way we follow Jesus.

Western quests are usually for knowledge. We say, "Knowledge is power," and we make it our goal in our educational institutions. But we ignore the spiritual reality that lies beneath the quest for knowledge. I have tried to show the important place of knowledge in relation to spiritual power. There is no doubt that knowledge is important. But its importance depends on how it is used. We must encourage spiritual leaders and cross-cultural workers to focus on the use of knowledge and its relationship to spiritual power, rather than on the knowledge itself.

Chapter 6

SATAN, THE COUNTERFEIT CONTEXTUALIZER

IN THE FIELD OF missiology, contextualization is seen as a positive, necessary part of cross-cultural ministry. It is an aspect of meeting people at the point of their felt needs in ways that are both relevant and biblical. Satan, however, can also be an excellent counterfeit "contextualizer," doing an expert job at meeting people at the point of their felt needs in culturally appropriate ways. The fact that he often does so through deceit is not usually recognized. I am told that there's a Japanese volcano where people have erected signs imploring the spirits not to allow it to erupt again. There are also shrines and a temple there at which visitors can add their petitions to those of decades' worth of earlier visitors. There may be less of a clear distinction in that language between the concepts of spirits and a high God, thus blurring any obvious difference between prayer to God and appeasement of spirits.

Satan counterfeits God's reality by producing religious systems that are quite logical once people believe the basic lie or deceit underlying them. With regard to reincarnation, likewise, he has long since convinced people of the logic of the recycling of persons. All he has to do in this matter is to assign demons to recount for people the details of the lives of real people who lived in the past, as if these lives were their own former lives. Very convincing, and very contextualized. What is more logical than to believe that people get recycled through reincarnation, once one has accepted ideas such as that one life is not enough to accomplish all that we're meant to accomplish, or that because the baby looks like deceased grandpa, he is a reincarnation of grandpa?

And, since people have such a felt need for spiritual power, how better to gain control of them than by giving certain of them (e.g., shamans) counterfeit power. Shamans, however, often know that in repayment for the use of that power during their lifetimes, they will die a horrible death. But they consider it worth the cost for the power and prestige they have been given.

In addition to these larger areas of satanic behavior, demonic beings are quite skilled at fulfilling "smaller" felt needs for such things as money, position, fame, control, revenge, and even a sense of security and love. But all have an eventual price tag attached.

I read a letter once from a woman who said she made a pact with the devil, bargaining for power, prestige, and wealth. She promised him in writing that if he would give her these things, she would give him her first son and every first son from then on in the families of her descendants. The report I heard was that it can be shown now, about three generations later, that each of the first sons in her family have suffered major problems of one sort or another—problems of the kind that lead one to suspect that the lady's pact with the devil is having an effect.

SATAN'S PREDICTABILITY

A principle that becomes apparent when we study the evil one is that the ways in which he works are quite predictable. Scripture indicates that angels are primarily servants and messengers of God. As such, they simply obey what God instructs them to do—they are not necessarily creative. So, assuming Satan and his "angels" are also uncreative and unoriginal, they spend their time counterfeiting and damaging those things that God has brought into existence. They can, however, influence humans who are creative and

SECTION ONE: BACKGROUND

thus, through deceit, gain some ability to originate. Whatever creativity Satan has, therefore, is stolen from the humans he deceives.

Though he depends on this stealing of human talents, his activities tend to be easily recognizable by those who understand the ways in which he works. For example, I have often been able to figure out how a demon has been functioning by simply asking myself the question, "If I were a demon (or Satan), what would I do in this situation?"[1]

Perhaps this is what Paul was getting at in 2 Cor 2:11 when he stated that "we know what [Satan's] plans [or devices or schemes] are." It is fairly obvious, for example, that he works in terms of human constants, such as pride and the desire for prestige, position, and power. He is active in promising such things, allowing good to happen for a time and then "closing in" on people, making them pay for whatever he has given them.

It is predictable that he will deceive people into believing his promises and accepting his gifts. He does this more often by telling partial and twisted truths than by obviously lying. His gifts, however, counterfeit the things God gives, since he has nothing of his own making to give. Thus, he counterfeits gifts of prophecy, knowledge, wisdom, tongues, as well as gifts of healing and even deliverance.

A large percentage of the world's population believe that ancestors continue to participate in human affairs. It is my working assumption that to be culturally relevant, Satan has assigned demons to impersonate those who have died. Once one has believed that ancestors remain a part of the living community after death, it is then easy to believe that negative things that happen today are the result of revenge taken by dissatisfied ancestors. Predictably, our enemy will always direct our attention or worship away from the Creator of all and instead to humans, spirits, or created objects (see Rom 1:16–25).

There are aspects of counterfeit practices and beliefs that are disturbingly similar to what God has revealed in Jesus Christ,

---

1. In his widely read fictional book *The Screwtape Letters*, C. S. Lewis gives insights into how demons might possibly think and make plans.

Satan, the Counterfeit Contextualizer

yet lead adherents away from a life-giving relationship with God through Christ. In addition, the practice of animism is amazingly similar worldwide, though found in a large variety of societies and peoples, which causes us to wonder if there is a single mind behind them.

Since Satan's objective is to counter God and disrupt his creation, it is predictable that he will attempt to turn good things into bad (or at least unattractive) things, make bad things worse, and trick people to pursue good things in excessive ways. In temptation, he seldom simply opposes things, choosing rather to raise questions about rightness, fairness, and the like, as he did in the garden of Eden. He prefers to work in terms of deceit rather than with outright lies.

Another predictable way that Satan works is to play off a human vulnerability by planting a deceit or a lie and then "training" humans to perpetuate that untruth themselves. Thus, the deceit on which reincarnation and communication with ancestors is based gets perpetuated within the human community generation after generation, probably without much help from satanic beings themselves. Since meanings are difficult to change (see chapter 7), the staying power of such lies is great.

So, in looking at Satan's activities cross-culturally, we need to look for many quite predictable patterns. We need to recognize, however, that these patterns will consist of the ways of thinking and behaving in the receptor society, whether or not they fit our own cultural logic. That is, Satan contextualizes his deceit. For example, in Western societies where people are quite often unaware of spiritual realities, Satan can impact lives through activities that many see as harmless: getting fortunes read, reading tarot cards, or consulting horoscopes when making a decision. Likewise, harm can be done through membership in what seem to be constructive organizations, such as Freemasonry or other quasi-religious groups that can appear erudite and innocent. In traditional family-oriented societies, what could be more logical than the satanic deception that one's ancestors are still alive and participating in the lives of their decedents? Or that it would be better to follow the assumed messages or practices of the ancestors than to receive the good news about Jesus being communicated? Or that people reincarnate after they die?

SECTION TWO

BASIC CONCEPTS

Chapter 7

FORMS, MEANINGS, AND EMPOWERMENT

A VERY IMPORTANT ISSUE in any discussion of the gospel in culture is the difference between cultural forms and their meanings. By "forms" we mean all the customs and structures, visible and invisible, that make up a culture. By "meanings" we mean the personal interpretations that yield a people's understanding of these forms. The forms are the parts of culture. The meanings exist not in the forms themselves but in the people who use the forms. Meanings are attached by people, according to the agreements of their group concerning what the forms signify.

By virtue of the fact that people participating in the same sociocultural group agree with each other on what significance to attach to each cultural form, they can communicate with each other. If they did not agree, they could not communicate. This is the problem with people who speak different languages. Though the members of each language group use essentially the same sounds, they organize them differently. Members of another language group, then, cannot even accurately interpret words that sound familiar to them, since they are not in on the agreements of the speakers of the first language. Though they have been taught to agree with the members of their language group what particular

SECTION TWO: BASIC CONCEPTS

combinations of sounds mean, they do not know what the agreements of the other group are unless they learn that language. Language learning, like all culture learning, is a matter of learning the agreements concerning meanings that the new group habitually attaches to the sound forms they use in speaking to each other.

A major problem in cross-cultural communication is the problem of changing the meanings of familiar forms. In seeking to assist people to accept and live out the gospel in terms of their own cultural forms, we are assisting them to use those forms for new purposes and, therefore, to attach new or modified meanings to them. When John the Baptist began to use baptism within the Jewish community to initiate people into his renewal movement, he was reinterpreting a form that was well known as a way of initiating gentile converts into Judaism. This cultural form was also used by Greek mystery religions as an initiation ceremony. When early Jesus communities decided to use it to signify initiation into a life of following Christ, they were largely following John's lead, since the earliest Jesus followers assumed that their faith was to remain within Judaism. When baptism was used in gentile Christian communities, the meaning was more in keeping with that signified by the use of baptism in the initiation of gentiles into Judaism. In either case, the meaning was in part the same as that of previous practice and in part a modification of that meaning. Jesus also took the Jewish Passover meal and reinterpreted it into what we call the Lord's Supper. In addition to these cultural forms, the early Jesus communities reinterpreted words such as *theos* (God), *ekklesia* (gathering/fellowship/church), *kurios* (Lord), *agape* (love), and a host of other Greek words.

But cultural forms can also be empowered by spirit beings. God regularly causes his power to flow through words such as "in Jesus' name" and the commands we give to demons. When such words are conveying God's power, we call them "empowered language forms." James recommends that we use anointing oil to bring healing to the sick (Jas 5:14). But if the oil is to be effective, it needs to be dedicated in the name of Jesus and thus empowered. The elements used in the Lord's Supper can (and should) also be

Forms, Meanings, and Empowerment

dedicated and empowered for specific purposes such as blessing and healing. Paul's handkerchiefs and aprons were empowered so that people received healing through them (Acts 19:12). It was likewise with Jesus' robe (Luke 8:43–48).

In some societies, people dedicate the things they make to spirits or gods, especially if those things are to be used for religious purposes or in situations involving risk or danger. In the South Pacific, for example, those who made the large canoes used for fishing or warfare regularly dedicated them to their gods. Even those who identify as Christians might still do this. When such things are dedicated to satanic spirits, they are empowered by those spirits.[1] Many missionaries and travelers who bought dedicated things and took them home have experienced difficulties because by putting those objects in their home, they have unwittingly invited in enemy spirits

Nevertheless, breaking the power of such objects is usually not difficult. Since we have infinitely more power in Jesus Christ than such objects can contain, we simply have to claim his power to break the enemy's power in the object. After claiming the power of Jesus to break enemy power in such objects, I usually go on to bless the object in the name of Jesus. The problem with satanic empowerment is not whether we have the power to break it, but rather overcoming our ignorance so that we recognize satanic dedication and know how to break it.

When bringing people to Christ, it is important to disempower anything that has been empowered with satanic power. Satanic power can be broken over empowered cultural forms such as rituals, buildings, carvings, songs, and any other custom or artifact a people wants to purify for God's use. Despite the fact that many counsel against using whatever the enemy has used, I believe we are to purify cultural forms, rather than reject them merely because our enemy has been using them. But we shouldn't try to use them until the power is broken. That would be unwise in the extreme.

---

1. See Woodberry, "Power and Blessing," for examples of empowered objects and places in Folk Muslim contexts.

SECTION TWO: BASIC CONCEPTS

The bigger problem is, however, the meaning problem. It may take two or three generations before the unredeemed meanings associated in people's minds with a given object can be fully replaced. New believers sometimes want to throw away every vestige of their culture that reminds them of their old involvement with shamans, rituals, and evil spirits. In their place, however, they tend to borrow foreign objects to which they often attach dubious meanings (such as sacredness because it is not understood). But foreign objects can falsely signal that God wants them to be foreigners in their own country, rather than show how their traditions can glorify Christ. As Western missionaries have so poorly understood the spiritual-power dimensions of the gospel, they have often encouraged other people to reject their culture and westernize. This dynamic has contributed to a form of following Jesus that is as powerless as faith often is in the West. Sadly, when this happens, the gospel looks irrelevant to many people except as it has provided such things as human status, prestige, and power.

We should not, however, give up, especially since the danger posed by secularization is so great. Though we have not, perhaps, learned very well how to build the short bridge between animism and following Jesus, we should have learned by now that a "secularized Christianity" (the form found in many Western countries and those impacted by Western missions) is a long way from the Bible in the area of spiritual power.

Chapter 8

CULTURAL CONSTANTS IN THE RELATIONSHIP BETWEEN SPIRIT AND HUMAN WORLDS

IN DEALING WITH SPIRITUAL power cross-culturally, there are a variety of basic principles to be made explicit. Among them is the scriptural fact that there is a close relationship between what goes on in human life and what goes on in the spirit realm.

To get a picture of this important fact, I like to think of reality as made up of two incredibly large and complicated layers. The basic layer (from our human point of view) is made up of all that happens in human life. The spirit level mirrors the human layer so that every human happening has a spiritual component. Thus, both God and his helpers, as well as Satan and his helpers, are involved in everything in the human realm.

All of a person's behavior happens on the lower layer and is mirrored on the upper (spiritual) layer. That is, all human behavior has a spiritual dimension, whether or not we are aware of it.

We learn from the discussion between God and Satan in the book of Job and from Jesus' statement that Satan wanted to sift the apostles like wheat (Luke 22:31–32) that Satan is anxious to assert himself to disrupt our lives. We learn from Dan 10:13 (an answer

SECTION TWO: BASIC CONCEPTS

to prayer delayed by a demonic being) and 2 Cor 4:4 (Satan blinding those who do not yet believe) that the enemy can sometimes be successful in thwarting God's plans. And we learn from the ministries of Jesus and his disciples that we can thwart at least some of the enemy's plans by casting demons out of people. In addition, the angels, and presumably demons as well, are watching us as we carry out our activities (Eph 3:10; 1 Tim 5:21; 1 Pet 1:12).

As in all of life, beyond the differences in cultural understandings and expression, there are basic aspects of our faith that are the same cross-culturally. In working with God, there are basics such as obedience to him, preceded by listening to him and following his word and his leading in our lives, and bringing freedom to captives. With regard to Satan's kingdom, there are basic aspects of how Satan attracts people, how he influences and oppresses them, and the kind of strategies he uses to keep them under his influence. In addition to these basics concerning God and Satan, there are certain basic aspects of human-being-ness relating to how we use our wills, our capability for relating to the spirit world, our vulnerability to temptation and deceit, and the like.

That both God and Satan work in partnership with people in terms of their culture is a constant we can expect to find in every cultural context. Underlying this reality is the fact that both God and Satan have plans for any given people and their culture and seek to accomplish those plans by working with human will. Though it is apparent that Satan is having great influence on the human scene, we learn from Scripture (especially the events surrounding Jesus' life, death, and resurrection) that God is working out his own purposes in the background and that Satan's ultimate defeat is certain. We, therefore, can expect to find both Satan and God working in every cultural context. Satan, of course, has his human representatives working hard to expand his kingdom or realm. We believe, however, that God is not inactive in any cultural situation. According to Rom 1:16–2:16, God is working in conscience and culture so that, whatever excuses those who choose Satan's way may give, they are accountable to God for their decisions.

It is important for us to look for God's working in the culture we are serving in, as well as be aware and watchful for Satan's working.

CULTURAL STRUCTURING

It is always important to distinguish cultural structure from the persons who operate that structuring. Contextualization studies usually focus on the structuring, leaving implicit the fact that it is people who produce and operate that structuring. Culture does not run itself. Culture simply lies there, like the roads we drive on. It is like the script of a play, memorized but regularly altered by the actors for a variety of reasons—some good, some bad, and most neutral.

In dealing with spiritual reality, it is important to recognize that we have both human persons and spirit beings involved in the way cultural structuring is used. Most cultural structuring is capable of being used either for good or for evil. Such things as status and prestige can be used by those who have them either to help others or to hurt them. The fact that there are differing levels of status and power may not be, in and of itself, a bad thing. Satan, however, entices people to use their status to hurt others, while God gently prods his people to use their status and the authority and power that goes with it to assist the powerless.

But in each case, the spiritual being (God or Satan) works with people in terms of the cultural structuring in which they are involved. In dealing with spiritual conflict, as with all studies of cultural behavior, our focus needs to be on people within culture and not simply on culture itself.

The importance of human habit must be recognized. Culture seems to have power over people because people follow cultural guidelines through force of habit. That is, the apparent power of culture is in reality the power of human habit. Thus, any attempts to change culture are really attempts to change human habits. The structuring is a function of the script produced by and followed, for the most part, by the actors out of habit (once they have memorized it). It is, however, often creatively changed by them—either because

SECTION TWO: BASIC CONCEPTS

they forgot, something didn't go as planned, or they simply chose to be creative. When we find enemy influence contextualized within sociocultural patterns and habitually followed, we appeal for people to change their habits so that they use either their present cultural patterns for godly purposes or change the patterns entirely. The point is that our appeal is always to people to change habits, with or without a change in cultural structure. We cannot appeal to an impersonal thing like a cultural structure or pattern.

Chapter 9

ANIMISM: SATAN'S COUNTERFEIT

SATAN COUNTERFEITS GOD'S CULTURAL behavior. Animism is a label that can describe a variety of spiritual and cultural forms and practices found in most tribal or folk religions as well as in the daily lives of many who self-identify as Muslim, Buddhist, Hindu, and even Christian. In many ways, animism attempts to counterfeit the spiritual power of faith in Christ.

There are many forms of animism. Some animists believe that each rock, tree, and physical entity contains its own spirits and that these spirits govern life. Animism is the belief—and accompanying practices—that the world is full of spirits that can hurt us unless we are careful to appease them.

Animists may or may not believe in a high god. When they do, the deity is usually seen as benign and thus in need of little, if any, attention. Animists agree, however, that the spirits need to be watched and kept happy, lest they hurt people. In addition, animists believe that evil spirits can inhabit material objects and places such as certain mountains (e.g., Old Testament high places), trees, statues (e.g., idols), rocks, rivers (e.g., the Ganges), territories, fetishes, charms, and any other thing or place that is dedicated to the spirits. Animists also believe in magic and the ability of at

SECTION TWO: BASIC CONCEPTS

least certain people to convey power via curses, blessings, spells, and the like.

The Bible teaches the validity of spiritual power and includes accounts of certain forms of spiritual power that appear similar to what is found in the practice of animism (e.g., power places such as the holy of holies; objects containing spiritual power such as the ark of the covenant, Moses' staff, or Jesus' robe; physical acts to acknowledge spiritual power such as the removal of shoes around the burning bush; the use of physical substances in healing and miracles such as mud or oil; and the like). Though these seem similar to animistic forms, with the true God as the source of power and the One who controls his power, biblical practice of spiritual power is vastly different from the practice of animism.

The difference between animism and faith in Christ is in the source of power. In areas such as healing, dedication, and blessing, Jesus followers and animists do essentially the same things, but the source of animist power is Satan and the source of power for Jesus followers is God. We learn both from Scripture and practical experience that many, if not all, of the rules that apply to God's interactions with humans also apply to the ways the enemy interacts with us.[1] For example, obedient partnership with God in prayer, worship, sacrifice, and service enables him to carry out his purposes in the world. On the other side, obedient partnership with Satan in these same ways enables him to accomplish his purposes. The importance of obedience in spiritual conflict is thus underlined.

We see that objects, such as idols or implements used in religious rituals, may be dedicated to gods or spirits and thus contain spiritual power. The Bible shows that objects can be dedicated to our God and thus convey his power (e.g., Paul's handkerchiefs, Moses' staff). On the surface, containing and conveying power look the same, especially since what animists believe to be power contained in objects is, in reality, satanic power conveyed by them.

For another example, animist diviners, shamans, and others can heal with the power of Satan. God can also heal by his own power. The fact that satanic healing leads sooner or later

---

1. Kraft, *Behind Enemy Lines*, ch. 2.

to captivity and misery is not immediately apparent to the one healed. More immediately obvious is the fact that God's healing leads to freedom and peace. But at first, both types of healing look similar, and people who seek healing rather than the Healer are easily deceived, especially since demons seem often to work faster than God does.[2]

Our authority as followers of Jesus, versus the authority Satan can give his followers, is an important issue at this point. Those who don't know the difference between God-given authority to work in spiritual power and the way animists work in spiritual power can assume that those working in God's power are practicing animism.[3]

But when we exercise the power and authority Jesus gives us to do things animists do (such as healing, casting out demons, blessing people and objects, dedicating buildings, praying for rain or against floods), we are not animists since we are working in submission to God, in God's power and not Satan's. We are simply exercising the authority Jesus taught his disciples to exercise (Luke 9:1), and encouraging all Jesus followers to do the same (Matt 28:19).

We may summarize some of the major issues in this discussion by means of the following chart, designed to show many of the contrasts between animism and God-given authority. Note again that the primary expressions of each of these areas will look very similar at the surface level. It is in the underlying power and motivations where they differ.

---

2. The appearance, at times, of the enemy working more quickly than God does is likely due to the fact that the enemy does not wait patiently to grant benefits in a way that is ultimately best for the person, but rushes in to deceive.

3. See Priest et al., "Missiological Syncretism."

SECTION TWO: BASIC CONCEPTS

	ANIMISM	GOD-GIVEN AUTHORITY
POWER	Believed to be contained in people and objects	God conveys his power through people and objects
NEED (in order to utilize spiritual power)	Felt need to learn how to manipulate spiritual power through magic or authority over spirits	We are to submit to God and learn to work with him in the exercise of power and authority from him
ONTOLOGY (what is really going on)	Power from Satan: he is the one who manipulates	Power from God: he empowers and lovingly uses us for his purposes
GOD	God is good but distant, therefore ignore him	God is good, therefore relate to him—he is close and involved with us
SPIRITS	To be feared and can hurt us, therefore appease them	They are defeated, therefore assert God's authority over them
PEOPLE	Victims of capricious spirits who never escape from being victims	They are captives, but we can assert Jesus' authority to free them
RESULT	Those who receive power from Satan suffer great tragedy later	Those who work with God experience love and power throughout life and eternity
HOPE	Temporary hope	We win

Chapter 10

ANIMISM DOES NOT SIMPLY GO AWAY

SOMETIMES IT IS SIMPLY assumed that as people grow in their relationship with Jesus, their cultural customs and beliefs just go away. But it hasn't happened this way in most of the world. The major spiritual impulse of the world is still the belief in a world of spirits and the practice of appealing to and appeasing them. This worldview runs through many majority-world societies, including those where most of the population identifies with one of the major world religions such as Hinduism, Shintoism, Buddhism, Islam, or Christianity.

One day in Nigeria, the shaman in our village lost his wife. She was still young but died very suddenly. It was a sad situation, but the village headmaster, one of the five people I was working with, saw in it a wonderful opportunity for demonstrating the gospel. He took the school drum and led his students down into the village and to the home of the shaman to participate in the funeral. As was the custom, the bereaved shaman was in isolation in his hut, and the villagers were dancing funeral dances to the beat of funeral drumbeats, working the grief out of their systems. When he heard that the schoolchildren had come, however, he broke the rules and came out of his hut to greet and thank them. "I never knew you cared," were his words.

The shaman was so impressed that he started to come to church to find out what was being taught that had resulted in the school children sharing his grief. But he soon stopped coming, probably because many of the congregants were also his clients! He could even point to pastors and other Christian leaders as those who came to him when they needed power. For there was little power in the new way of the Christian faith that they had embraced. And it was the spiritual power that the shaman could wield that made him more important in the lives of the people than what the church stood for.

While the love, joy, and peace from their relationship with Jesus was valuable to the people, spiritual power was their number-one quest, and they found little or none of it in the Christian faith they had embraced. Though spiritual-power needs were constantly of concern to them, we missionaries came with medical practitioners who could dispense medicine or even perform surgery but knew little or nothing about how to work with the spiritual climate in which the people lived. We had been training church leaders to preach, but not to free people from spirits and diseases.

In Luke 11:20, Jesus says that the casting out of demons is proof that the kingdom has come to those we minister to. But if demons are ignored, what does that say about our attempts to serve in the kingdom?

There are things I learned as a missiologist long after my time in Nigeria when I could have helped the leaders I worked with in dealing with the spirit world. I did get to go back to do a brief seminar after I had gone through a kind of conversion myself into working in God's power to heal. I found at that time that my Nigerian hearers tracked very well with my teaching and practicing on dealing with the spirit world in the power of the Holy Spirit.

Witchcraft is a major problem in many parts of the world. Cross-cultural workers need to be able to detect it and deal with it when it occurs. In addition, they need to minister to people who are frightened by occult[1] practitioners and threats of witchcraft.

Occult practitioners are people who have given allegiance to Satan and work in Satanic power to carry out Satan's wishes. They usually operate in secret, empowered by Satan to thwart God's activities. They may give curses and satanic blessings. Christ followers, however, have the power to confront and break the power of whatever occult practitioners assert.

Fear of witchcraft is a major tactic of the enemy, and he uses fear to deceive people into thinking occult practitioners have more power than they really do. People may overreact and do foolish things in their attempts to get rid of whatever they believe is a result of occult activities. These practitioners may have real power, but they cannot outpower Jesus.

In Western societies, the activities of occult practitioners are more and more visible. Possible signs include the availability of resources for dabbling in witchcraft, and radio and social media advertisements for psychics, palm readers, and other practitioners where people are consciously or unconsciously exposed to satanic power. Along with these examples, some of the activities of Freemasonry, Scientology, and other groups could be categorized as "Western animism"—that is, the same type of manipulation of the spiritual realm as is found in animism practiced in majority-world societies.

We are in conflict with Satan and his demons, and we need to know what is going on and how to counteract it. We need to be receptor-oriented in responding to the spiritual-power concerns of different people groups around the world.

---

1. By "occult" I mean the practice of engaging with, relying upon, controlling, appeasing, or receiving benefits from what the Bible defines as evil spirits (though these spirits are not necessarily seen as evil by those relating to them).

Chapter 11

SPIRITUAL POWER IN BALANCE

IN ANY DISCUSSION ABOUT dealing with spiritual power, we need to keep our focus balanced. We have spoken in a previous chapter of the need for contextualizers to do their work in three crucial dimensions. As pointed out there, these dimensions are (1) our allegiance/relationship to Christ with all the love and obedience that entails, (2) the understanding that comes from continually experiencing his truth, and (3) the spiritual power Jesus gives us to use, as he did, in expressing his love and bringing freedom to others.

Spiritual power in Scripture, though prominent, is never an end in and of itself. It must always be balanced by concern for our relationship with God and for God's truth. When Jesus' followers came back from a power-filled excursion into the towns and villages of Galilee, reporting with excitement that "even the demons obeyed us when we gave them a command in your name" (Luke 10:17), Jesus cautioned them and pointed them to something more important. That more-important thing is our relationship with the God who provides the power. According to Jesus, this relationship resulting in our names being written in heaven (Luke 10:20) is to be a greater cause of rejoicing than even our power over demons.

As crucial as the power issue is, the relationship issue is even more important. In focusing on spiritual power, we must be careful

Spiritual Power in Balance

not to de-emphasize or neglect all the love and other fruits of the Spirit that a relationship with God entails.

Nor dare we neglect the issue of truth. Jesus spent most of his time teaching, demonstrating, and leading his followers into truth. In keeping with the implications of the Greek word for truth, this is to be an experienced truth, not simply intellectual truth. That continual experiencing of the truth, then, leads to ever-deepening understanding of the truth dimension of the gospel, as well as the power and relationship dimensions.

This experienced-truth dimension is based on obedience to Jesus within the relationship (John 8:31–32). And all bearing of fruit, including the fruit of spiritual power, is dependent on our abiding in Christ (John 15:1–17). We are, then, to minister to people in contextually appropriate ways with a balance of allegiance, truth, and power.[1] Any approach to the gospel that neglects or ignores any of these three dimensions is an incomplete and unbalanced faith.

Though, as mentioned, evangelical Christianity has usually been deficient in dealing with spiritual power, it has been strong on the truth dimension. And it has focused to some extent on allegiance and relationship, though this dimension has often been treated largely as a by-product of truth and knowledge. Pentecostal and charismatic strains of Christianity have often been more relevant to the peoples of the majority world due to their emphasis on spiritual power. Yet these expressions have their own drawbacks, and associated past mission efforts have not always shown respect toward the cultures of the receptor peoples.

When we look at these three dimensions in relation to Western evangelical missions, we come up with a chart such as the following:

	ALLEGIANCE	TRUTH	POWER
TRADITIONAL RELIGION	Wrong Allegiance	Counterfeit Truth	Satanic Power
WESTERN CHRISTIANITY	True Allegiance	God's Truth	
BIBLICAL FAITH IN CHRIST	True Allegiance	God's Truth	God's Power

1. See Kraft, "What Kind of Encounters."

SECTION TWO: BASIC CONCEPTS

Since the power dimension has not been adequately dealt with by the advocates of (Western) Christianity, people often continue to go to their traditional sources of power, even though they have pledged allegiance to Christ and are learning biblical truth. Any attempt to rectify this situation must apply biblical emphasis and guidelines to the missing dimension.

Chapter 12

TWO LEVELS OF CONFLICT

SPIRITUAL CONFLICT (I.E., SPIRITUAL warfare) happens on at least two levels. The lower level is what I call "ground-level conflict." The upper level, then, is what I call the "cosmic-level conflict" (called "strategic-level warfare" by Wagner).[1] Ground-level conflict involves dealing with spirits (demons) that oppress persons. My experience would suggest that personal spirits or demons are of at least three kinds: family, occult, and "ordinary."

Ground-Level Spirits (oppressing people)
1. Family Spirits: resulting from dedications to family gods (named deities associated with and appeased by extended families)
2. Occult Spirits: resulting from direct allegiances with spirits to obtain benefits
3. Ordinary Spirits: attached to oppressive attitudes and emotions

Family and occult demons usually seem to be stronger than the ordinary demons, but dealing with them is essentially the same as dealing with ordinary demons. Family and occult spirits gain their power through conscious or unconscious dedication to them. They, then, are passed down from generation to generation

---

1. Wagner and Greenwood, "Strategic-Level Deliverance Model," 173–98.

SECTION TWO: BASIC CONCEPTS

even after the practice of dedication has ceased (e.g., after a person has decided to follow Christ). Ordinary spirits empower emotions such as fear, shame, and anger. They also attach to problems such as lust, suicide, rebellion, and many others. In each case, demons can only influence people by legal right. Rights are given through such means as dedications and wallowing in sinful emotions. There is a human cause that gives the spirits access.

At the cosmic level, there are at least five kinds of higher-level spirits that I have labeled: territorial, institutional, vice, nature/household/cultural-item, and ancestral.

Cosmic-Level Spirits (in the air, Eph 2:2)
1. Territorial Spirits: spirits over regions and cities such as those over nations mentioned in Dan 10:13, 21 (called "Prince of Persia" and "Prince of Greece")
2. Institutional Spirits: assigned to churches, governments, educational institutions, occult organizations, religions, temples, shrines
3. Vice Spirits: oversee and encourage systemic sins such as racism, exploitation, injustice, prostitution, gambling, pornography, war
4. Nature, Household, and Cultural-Item Spirits: residing in trees, rivers, homes, dedicated work implements, music, rituals, artifacts used in power practices
5. Ancestral Spirits: associated with entire ethnic groups, believed by many peoples to be their physically dead ancestors who still participate in the activities of the living community

My personal experience has led me to surmise that the cosmic-level spirits are apparently in charge of ground-level spirits, assigning them to people and supervising them as they carry out their assignments against people to tempt, harass, and oppress.

Jesus, of course, frequently encountered and cast out ground-level demons. The evidence that he dealt with higher-level spirits is, however, slim, except in his encounter with Satan himself (Luke 4:1–13). I suspect, though, that in confronting and defeating Satan in his own territory (i.e., the wilderness was considered the property of Satan), Jesus broke much of Satan's power over at least that part of Palestine. And some have suggested that the demons afflicting the Gerasene demoniac (Luke 8:26–33) were territorial spirits. If so, they were concentrated in one man, like ground-level demons, and dealt with in the same way Jesus dealt with those whose assignment was purely ground level.

Discussions of the contextualization of biblical understandings of the spirit world and spiritual conflict need to take into account these levels of spirits and what to do about them.

COSMIC-LEVEL SPIRITS

Animists believe there are specific spirits attached to nations, regions, mountains, rivers, and other geographical features. We find this understanding in the Old Testament, where the Baal gods were considered to have control of the plains, while Yahweh was supposed to be merely a mountain god. In the events recorded in 1 Kgs 20:23–30, we see Yahweh angered at this belief on the part of the Syrians and, therefore, giving Israel a victory on the plains.

One of the spin-offs of the belief in territorial spirits is the understanding that when a person enters the territory of a given god, he needs to show respect to that god. In the Old Testament we continually find Israel honoring the Baals and other gods when they were in territory they believed to belong to these gods. See, for example, Hos 2:8 where Israel attributed their prosperity to the Baal gods in the area. In order to cement relationships with the surrounding countries, Solomon married wives from Ammon, Moab, Edom, and other places, and he erected altars to their gods to show honor to their countries. In this way, he kept peace with these countries by keeping the wives and their relatives happy (1 Kgs 11:1–10). But he sacrificed the favor of Yahweh.

Westerners tend to feel that such beliefs about territorial spirits need not be taken seriously, since we believe that these so-called gods are imaginary beings empowered only by superstition. The Bible, however, shows God and his people taking such spirits seriously. In fact, we are warned against giving them honor or fearing them, since the true God is greater and more powerful than these servants of Satan. And, if we are properly related to the true God,

SECTION TWO: BASIC CONCEPTS

we have the authority to protect ourselves from other gods and to confront and defeat them when necessary.

It is my position that people who have been under the sway of territorial spirits for generations have a great deal of understanding of what territory the spirits have influence over and the results of this influence. Any approach to the gospel in such areas, therefore, will need to recognize the reality of the spirits over the area and gain understanding of their assignments. We will then have to deal with them by taking away their rights as we work with the true God to retake territory that is rightfully his.[2]

Experiments in Argentina and elsewhere in the world suggest that a direct approach to fighting against cosmic-level spirits can be successful. Similar to ground-level conflict, however, it is most important to clear out the spiritual "corporate garbage."[3] Thus, issues of confession of sin, repentance, reparation, reconciliation, and unity are the first order of business if our praying against territorial bondage is to be successful. The chapter by Ed Silvoso in my book *Behind Enemy Lines* reports on the success of such an approach in Resistencia, Argentina, where Silvoso led a three-year comprehensive spiritual attack aimed at breaking the power of the territorial spirits over the city and opening the people up for evangelism. That approach involved getting the pastors (the spiritual "gatekeepers") to repent of their sins and disunity and to unite. Pastors and lay church leaders were trained in spiritual-conflict praying, repentance, reconciliation, prayer marching, and, after two years of such preparation, all-out evangelism. The results have been spectacular.

Some have criticized such efforts to engage in cosmic-level conflict, pointing out that Jesus never seemed to concern himself

---

2. See Wagner, *Engaging the Enemy*, for case studies dealing with territorial spirits.

3. In inner-healing prayer, I refer to "rats and garbage"—rats being like demons and garbage being like what attracts demons, such as pain, trauma, fear, sin, pride, etc. When the "garbage" is renounced and healing comes, the "rats" can more quickly be given orders to leave. When praying over areas, "corporate garbage" can be renounced and healed, and cosmic-level spirits can be more readily dealt with.

with any level above ground level. Could it be, though, that the Holy Spirit is simply leading us in our day into more of the "all truth" that Jesus promised in John 16:13? And might it be that by cleaning up so much of the ground-level garbage and praying as much as he did in private, as well as in John 17, Jesus was contributing greatly to the breaking of satanic power at the cosmic level? In addition, Jesus' direct confrontation with Satan in the desert certainly must have involved the powers at a cosmic level. People engaged in cosmic-level conflict are discovering that most of what it takes to effectively confront higher-level spirits takes place at ground level. I am referring to such things as confession of sin, repentance, reconciliation, and the need for spiritual gatekeepers to work in unity.

Whether or not strategies to confront cosmic-level spirits are scriptural, we cannot argue against the basis in Scripture for repentance, unity, and intercessory prayer, which often provide the key to breaking the power of higher-level spirits. Disunity, lack of repentance, and failure to fast and pray may be seen as the cosmic-level garbage on which cosmic-level rats feed.

An important technique developed by cosmic-level conflict practitioners such as John Dawson, Ed Silvoso, and C. Peter Wagner is called "Spiritual Mapping."[4] This is an approach to discerning and identifying the cosmic spirits that operate over the areas charted in the preceding section as a step toward developing strategies to oppose and defeat them.

Spiritual mapping is much like what God told Moses to do when he commanded him to send spies into the promised land to learn about the situation that Israel would face as they attempted to take the land. Such spying is a regular feature in warfare and helps develop the strategies for attacking the enemy. It should certainly be a part of any attempt to conduct cosmic-level spiritual conflict.

---

4. See Dawson, *Taking Our Cities for God*; Silvoso, "Prayer Power in Argentina"; Wagner, *Engaging the Enemy* and *Breaking Strongholds*.

SECTION THREE

SPECIFIC ISSUES

Chapter 13

DEMONIZATION

AN IMPORTANT ISSUE TO deal with in every society is ground-level demonization. We should expect that a significant percentage of people (including many Christians) will be oppressed by demons, especially in societies where babies are dedicated to spirits or gods. How demons behave in any given society and the differences in demonic activity between societies are fitting subjects for research in this area.

At ground level, the casting out of demons under the authority of Jesus Christ appears to be cross-culturally valid. Though I have seldom been able to simply command demons out as easily as the Gospels seem to show Jesus doing, I have been successful in confronting and defeating them in Jesus' name in several different cultural contexts.

My experience in ministering to demonized people of other societies leads me to conclude that the basic principle of "dual causation" is cross-culturally valid. This principle holds that demons can heavily influence a person only if there are factors with that person that give them a legal right. The dual causation, then, is to recognize that there is both a human cause (the internal issue to which the demons are attached) and a spirit cause (the demons

SECTION THREE: SPECIFIC ISSUES

themselves). Dealing with demons in people of other societies requires us to address the internal problems as well.

The analogy I use is to say that demons are like rats, and rats live where there is garbage. Demonic rats gain their rights and their strength from the human, spiritual, mental, and emotional garbage in the life of the persons they oppress. There is also inherited garbage, such as dedication to spirits. An example of mental garbage is believing lies. Emotional garbage can include wallowing in fear, anger, shame, hatred, or lust. Carrying such garbage gives demons entrance, allows them to stay, and gives them power.

Clearing out the garbage in people is the most important aspect of the process of fighting demons at ground level. Demons must have legal rights to attach to people. Those rights are a function of the garbage. The garbage, therefore, is much more important to clear out than the demons. However, if the person is to get well, both problems must be dealt with. When the garbage is cleared out first, the demons are weakened and go quietly when they are challenged.[1] They seldom, if ever, leave on their own, though—they usually need to be ordered to leave. We will see below that this rats-and-garbage principle also applies to cosmic-level spirits.

As mentioned previously, our enemy is good at contextualizing. He will adapt his approach to the problems and concerns most prominent in any given society. A major part of his strategy is to be able to do his work without being noticed, especially in areas where there might be Jesus followers who know how to combat demonization. Making negative things worse and getting people to go overboard on positive things are some of his preferred ways of working. Yet the things he pushes in each society will differ for maximum effectiveness in Satan's attempts to deceive and disrupt.

In cultures where the relationship between a mother-in-law and a daughter-in-law is particularly difficult, demons will often be active in pushing mothers-in-law to be oppressive and daughters-in-law to hate them. In some traditional societies with a strong fear of the unknown, demons will push all the buttons they can to increase the fear and the practice of going to diviners (where

---

1. See Kraft, *Defeating Dark Angels*.

demonic influence is increased) for relief. In patriarchal societies, where male domination of women and children is strongly inculcated, the enemy kingdom is very active in increasing the abuse and pain of women and children. And many parts of the world have satanic enhancement of racism and social class oppression. The thing that all such examples have in common is that the seed from which Satan works to produce harmful fruit is always culturally relevant.

With regard to techniques people use for dealing with demons, the enemy is also active in deception. Deliverance sessions in some communities have involved beating the demonized person to get the demons out. Such attempts at deliverance may thus be orchestrated by Satan himself. I know of two situations in which demonized people were killed as a result of such beatings, thus fulfilling a demon's intent to destroy those he oppresses.

The appropriate and proper approach to getting people free from demons in any society seems to involve clearing out the spiritual and emotional garbage to weaken the demons and then kicking them out. Fighting physically with them is never a good idea. And even when it is necessary to physically restrain a demonized person, it is God's power wielded through words, not physical force, that gets the demons out.

Though I have found this approach to be cross-culturally valid, there can be problems. People from honor-shame cultures often find it very difficult to admit things that they have done or said that have given rights to the demons. There often is a worldview belief that if a problem is hidden or denied, it will simply go away if one waits long enough. This is not true. In fact, the longer people hold on to deep problems, the more such problems can fester deep inside of them and affect their present lives.

Since God is a God of truth, no matter what the culture, people need to "come clean" and be willing to process the things they have done and that have been done to them if they are to be healed. And this is true no matter how culturally strange it might be for people to admit these disagreeable things and to forgive those who have hurt them. The reactions to things done to them

SECTION THREE: SPECIFIC ISSUES

must also be addressed, in order that the heavy emotional loads such reactions produce may be brought to Christ and laid at his feet (Matt 11:28). The hurtful events cannot be changed. What happened, happened. But, with the help of Jesus, reactions such as rage, bitterness, fear, and especially unforgiveness can be given to Jesus, bringing emotional healing. When such things are brought to Christ, the demons have nothing more to cling to and are easily banished.

Chapter 14

DEALING WITH INHERITED FAMILY OR OCCULT SPIRITS AND GENERATIONAL SPIRITUAL INHERITANCE

WE NEED TO LEARN about the conditions under which demons are passed on to the next generation of those dedicated to the spirits, usually at birth. It is the custom for many of the world's peoples to dedicate their children at birth. Thus, spiritual bondage can be passed on from generation to generation. We need to claim the authority and power of Jesus to cancel all of the enemy's rights in people's lives through spiritual dedication. This sets captives free from generational bondage and brings a basic freedom that many of the world's peoples need to receive.

Several years ago I was working to bring inner healing, including freedom from some demons, to an Asian Christian cross-cultural worker in her fifties. In addition to the fairly normal problems to which demons were attached, such as hatred and anger, she was oppressed by family demons that she had inherited from her parents. These, then, had been strengthened when her parents dedicated her at a temple soon after her birth and when they took her to a temple as a child for healing. She was also carrying demons that entered when she was involved in practicing martial arts under a master who, without her awareness, dedicated all he did to demonic spirits. She had no idea that these things that had happened long ago could be responsible for the daily (and nightly) torment she experienced. She understood the reality of demons but had, until recently, been believing the lie that demons could not attach to Christians (especially dedicated ones such as those who served as cross-cultural workers).

My experience in ministry with East Asian families has taught me about child dedications. The name, date, and time of the baby's birth can be written down and taken to be registered with the gods of the temple. Though many families claim not to believe in spirits anymore, such registration is sometimes done "just in case." These dedications allow spirits to attach to the child and also empower any inherited family spirits.

It is usually easy to break the power of even long-standing family demons, since the power of Jesus is so great. We simply claim Jesus' authority over the vows, curses, dedications, sins, and any other ways in which rights have been given to demons by ancestors, the afflicted person, or anyone in authority over the person. Then the work of deliverance can proceed to dealing with demons attached to emotional reactions, such as anger, hatred, unforgiveness, and fear. Once each of the areas of demonic permission has been addressed, the demons go quietly at our command.

There may be family spirits in anyone who is within three or four generations of the routine dedications to gods or spirits, or anyone who has received healing from such spirits. Consequently, anyone within three or four generations of involvement with these practices could be carrying family spirits or occult spirits. Various belief systems could promote allegiance to various family or occult spirits as well.

Like family spirits, occult spirits can be inherited down to at least the third or fourth generation and probably longer in some cases. Even if a person has never been involved in an occult organization, they could still carry a demon from a previous source in their family, such as a parent or grandparent's involvement with the occult. Occult spirits are dealt with in the same way as family spirits. We look for the curses, dedications, and other entry points that give the demons rights. Then we break their power and cast the demons out.

Chapter 15

GODS, IDOLS, AND DIVINATION

THERE IS A STRONG negative tone in God's pronouncements concerning compromise with other gods and spirits, as well as the ways their power is engaged. I want to point to several of the prohibited areas and then discuss what may be done about them.

God's ideals in this area are quite clear from Scripture. The Old Testament, especially, is an excellent source to learn what is and is not allowable. Most of today's peoples share with the peoples of biblical times the understanding that the world is populated by evil spirits and that higher-level spirits are in charge of territory (see Dan 10:13, 21). God never counters that belief.

However, God is very much against his people honoring these spirits when it is assumed, as in both biblical times and most present societies, that when we enter the territory of any given spirit, we should be polite and recognize that spirit's right to control the territory. Indeed, God got quite angry and taught the people a lesson when it was assumed that he was only powerful in the mountains but not on the plains (1 Kgs 20:23–30).

The Bible is clear that the worship of any god but the true God is not permitted. We are to "worship no god but [Yahweh]" (Exod 20:3). There are to be no idols made or worshiped as God says, "I am the Lord your God and I tolerate no rivals" (Exod 20:5).

Gods, Idols, and Divination

And among the warnings in the New Testament is the command at the end of 1 John: "My children, keep yourselves safe from false gods!" (1 John 5:21).

Perhaps the clearest indication of what God feels about his people having relationships with other gods is found in the story of the people of Israel at Peor in Num 25. God became very angry at the Israelite leaders who attended feasts with Moabite women "where the god of Moab was worshiped" and where "the Israelites ate the food and worshiped the god Baal of Peor" (vv. 2–3). God was so angry at them that he commanded that those who had participated in that worship be killed publicly (v. 4). Then, when an Israelite man openly challenged the prohibition by taking a Midianite woman into his tent, God commended Phinehas, Aaron's grandson, for killing both the man and the woman saying,

> Because of what Phinehas has done, I am no longer angry with the people of Israel . . . [and] . . . he and his descendants are permanently established as priests, because he did not tolerate any rivals to me and brought about forgiveness for the people's sin. (vv. 11, 13)

Idolatry, then, is forbidden by God. Several other practices are also forbidden for God's people and labeled as the reasons why God drove out the inhabitants of Canaan. Deuteronomy 18:9–13 lists and labels several acts of idolatry as "disgusting practices." They are: sacrificing children, divination, looking for omens, using spells or charms, and consulting spirits of the dead.

So it is clear that many common traditional practices involving spiritual power are forbidden. God does not tolerate appeasing other gods or spirits or seeking information, health, wealth, or blessing from them. God's answer to the quest for these things is that we relate to him and allow him to take care of the opposing spirits and provide the blessings we need.

What God says to today's dual-allegiance Christians is serious. Many Christians find so little spiritual power in the gospel they know that they regularly seek help from forbidden power sources.

In many parts of the world, the kind of faith that Christians have received has been strong on the intellectual and spiritual

SECTION THREE: SPECIFIC ISSUES

distinctives of Western evangelical Christianity but virtually powerless in areas such as healing, deliverance, blessing, and the other areas traditionally covered by traditional practitioners and shamans (e.g., dedications, shrines, amulets). So, failing to find these needs met within their faith, Christians (including many pastors and other church leaders) have continued to go to traditional power brokers.

I trust, though, that God takes into account the ignorance of such people, and the ignorance of those who have shared the gospel about Jesus with them. We find in 2 Kgs 5 that God does take traditional authority relationships into account on at least one occasion. After Naaman was healed and committed himself to the God of Israel, he asked the prophet Elisha how he should now behave when he is required by his master to accompany him to a traditional temple. Naaman says, "I hope that the Lord will forgive me when I accompany my king to the temple of Rimmon, the god of Syria, and worship him" (v. 18). Elisha simply says, "Go in peace" (v. 19), indicating that God will understand and not hold it against Naaman.

Though God allowed Israel's belief in many gods to continue for some time, God insisted that there be no compromise with regard to allegiance—no rivals. Contacting spirits or dead people was totally prohibited. On the other hand, places of worship and even some rituals and transition rites, such as circumcision and baptism, that were previously used, can be reinterpreted, purified, and used to honor the true God. This is what Israel did with former worship rituals and ceremonies and the use of high places—they became places to worship the one true God, and perform the ritual sacrifices that he commanded.

The religious customs of the early Israelites nearly all came from their background and were purified and revised for Yahweh. Early Jesus followers had a number of customs from traditional roots as well, including baptism, requirements for spiritual leaders (listed in 1 Tim 3:1–13 and Titus 1:6–9), and important theological words (e.g., lord, fellowship/church, grace).

Chapter 16

ANCESTORS AND REINCARNATION

GIVEN THE CONCERN OF family members for those who have died, what a stroke of genius on the part of Satan to convince people that their loved ones still actively participate in human life. By doing so, demons are able to work more freely, disguised as spirits of ancestors. And since they already know things about that ancestor, they can do an excellent job of impersonation and, in the process, exert a great amount of control over people. Demons posing as ancestor spirits can bind people to false beliefs and rituals in a most impressive way.

Most of the peoples of the world have long since bought the lie that it is really their loved ones who are receiving and responding to their attentions and communications. And it is not easy for them to understand that what they have been believing for generations is a lie. Nor is it easy for academics who, with no experience with the demonic world themselves, argue interminably on the basis of pure theory about whether or not ancestors, demons, or Satan are real. Our enemy has done a good job of confusing them also. Unfortunately, then, the academics' lack of agreement affects the practitioners and would-be practitioners, causing doubt and

SECTION THREE: SPECIFIC ISSUES

uncertainty in their efforts to teach and minister against evil spiritual forces posing as ancestors.

Among the arguments suggesting that ancestors are really conscious of what is going on in human life and are present to influence it involve particular interpretations of the passage concerning King Saul's excursion to the medium in Endor (1 Sam 28:3–19) and the fact that at the transfiguration, Moses and Elijah appeared to Jesus (Luke 9:28–31). These passages, however, are best interpreted as specific times when God allowed deceased people to return for specific purposes. They have nothing to do with the possibility that ancestors are regularly conscious of and interacting with human life. More to the point is the statement in Heb 12:1 that "we have this large crowd of witnesses round us." But, though this verse may mean that the deceased are able to observe certain aspects of life on earth, it gives no indication that they can participate in human life.

So, we are left scripturally with no encouragement to believe that the dead interact with the living. And, in fact, we are warned sternly not to attempt to contact the dead (Lev 19:31; Deut 18:11). The practice of diviners seeking information about this life, and especially about the future from the deceased, is well-known in both Scripture and contemporary societies. It is a form of divination called "necromancy." God views this practice as "detestable"; Deut 18:12 describes this in the strongest of terms.

When ancestors are regarded as participants in the living community, people are being deceived and often oppressed. But how can we urge them to consider the biblical point of view? When people have for generations sought to communicate with ancestors, the complexity of how to present the gospel increases greatly.

"Where are my ancestors now?" they ask, often adding that their deepest desire is to be with them for eternity. With regard to where the ancestors are, I believe God's words to Abraham apply when he asked, "Will not the God of all the universe do right?" (Gen 18:25). Concerning relatives who have died, Jesus tells a parable of a rich man and his servant Lazarus (Luke 16:19–31), where the rich man who has died and was not merciful to Lazarus who was poor, suffered after death for his disobedience. The rich man in the story wanted his living descendants to listen to God and be warned.

To free people spiritually from satanic deception in ancestral matters, we will have to deal with demonization early on. Any commitment to enemy spirits is an invitation for the spirits to live inside. If this commitment has been going on for generations, with accompanying dedications of each newborn baby to the spirits, what we are dealing with are inherited spirits from a person's parents. These generational spirits need to be banished. So do any spirits inhabiting paraphernalia associated with the worship of ancestral spirits.

The challenges involved in changing cultural practices and meaning are another matter. Will people agree to speak to Jesus, asking him to convey any messages he chooses to our ancestors? Will people consider asking God to lead them regarding any symbol or practice that would be best to change or replace? Will the meanings be sufficiently changed? Are the experiments in Papua New Guinea that present Jesus as the Great Ancestor working? And are they theologically valid? We need to hear of more experiments in this area.

We learn from Scripture what God's ideal belief is. What, though, do we learn of his method of bringing about the necessary changes of worldview to lead to his ideal? I believe we get a clue from God's statement in Gen 20: "no other gods before me." That verse implies the existence of other gods and that they actually exist, but God is number one. This is God's starting point. Later, though, Paul states that though there are so-called gods, for his people there is but one God (1 Cor 8:1–6). I believe God is willing to start with a belief in many gods, placing himself above the others, but he helps those who start with this position (called henotheism) to grow to a "there are no other gods" position.

REINCARNATION OF ANCESTORS

In a time of prayer for healing, I directed a question to a demon who had been oppressing the person I was praying for. I asked if reincarnation was one of the things they did to deceive people. He answered something like, "Of course. We know people's lives in detail. It's easy for us to simply tell people someone else's life as if it was their own past life." This is how they fool Hindus into philosophizing about the recycling of lives or fool Westerners into believing something that is new in the West. As in many of Satan's activities, he has trained them to perpetuate his deceit themselves, without much, if any, of his help.

The Scripture is clear that "everyone must die once, and after that be judged by God" (Heb 9:27). There is, therefore, no scriptural allowance for anyone to be reborn into another earthly existence. God has created each of us unique and eternal. Therefore this belief, like idolatry and divination, cannot be contextualized and accepted. Dealing with any demons of reincarnation may be the first step toward freeing people from this lie.

Chapter 17

SHRINES AND DEDICATED PLACES

IT IS IMPORTANT THAT we recognize Satan's ability to heal and give benefits to those who come to places dedicated to him. For too long we have tried to ignore Satan's counterfeiting and the attraction it has for many who seek enough spiritual power to enable them to live their lives reasonably well.

Lands, buildings, rituals, music, and other geographical and cultural phenomena are routinely dedicated to gods and spirits. These dedications can be broken and dedication to God be substituted.

I stood with a Japanese friend at a Shinto shrine one day. As people entered and poured water over the statue there, we asked them what it was they sought. They said blessings for marriage and school examinations, healing of various ailments and relationships, fertility for themselves or loved ones, and other such things. As I stood there, I thought: Jesus is concerned about all of these things. How great it would be if the churches sponsored shrines where people could receive prayer in Jesus' name for such requests. Japanese people are used to going to places of power at times convenient to them rather than at set times such as Sunday morning. Even if such needs are prayed for in church (and they often are

SECTION THREE: SPECIFIC ISSUES

not), shrines where prayer is lifted up to God in Jesus' name would be more culturally appropriate places to care for them.

Such shrines would, of course, differ in several respects from normal Shinto shrines. For one thing, the land on which they stand would be spiritually cleansed of any evil spiritual powers and dedicated to God. In addition, such shrines would involve people who would pray for those who come, not simply a statue to pour water over. And it would be recommended at these shrines that those with further interest attend regular meetings (Sundays and other days) sponsored by believers. There would be literature as well, and the shrines would be advertised, as other shrines are, on the trains. And those who pray for people could be young people, thus giving the youth a ministry to serve in, for which they would usually have to wait till they got older.

These shrines can meet people's power needs. They would not look like foreign incursions into Japanese life that dispense knowledge about a foreign religion. Instead they would look like places of power, places where people go to seek answers in traditional ways.

Such an approach might be suggested for other areas of the world as well. Many of the world's peoples are accustomed to frequenting shrines to satisfy their quest for spiritual power. In some Muslim countries, it is customary for people to seek spiritual power at the tombs of saints (even Hindu saints!). For outreach, might some adaptation of that custom be appealing to the people of those areas?

Wherever such an approach is attempted, of course, the land and any buildings will have to be spiritually cleansed and then blessed with the power of Jesus. Traditional customs for dedicating buildings and property are likely to be adaptable for such purposes, but the power behind the dedications would be that of the true God.

Chapter 18

BLESSING, CURSING, AND SOUL TIES

SPIRITUAL POWER CONVEYED EITHER positively or negatively by words is likened by the apostle James to the rudder of a ship that, though small, wields a lot of power (Jas 3:4–11). We are cautioned to pay careful attention to the words we speak.

In traditional societies people are more serious about the power of words. When my wife was doing research among the Navajo, she noticed great fear in the interviewee concerning even the mention of evil powers without claiming God's power and protection first. A time of prayer proclaiming God's protection and the indwelling power of the Holy Spirit was necessary.

Cross-cultural workers need to know the power of blessing and use it regularly. When we bless, God empowers our words, and a spiritual transaction takes place. As with curses, the person who puts on the blessing or curse owns it and can remove it (Luke 10:6–11).

Cursing is very frequent. There are informal curses invoked through words of anger or hatred toward others. There are more formal curses where a shaman takes some item pertaining to a person (e.g., hair, clipped nails), a possession, or a doll image of a person and utters ritualized curses on that person. The breaking of informal curses may come more easily; the breaking of formal curses may need more intense renouncement and prayer.[1]

The person who puts the curse on owns the curse and can remove it by renouncing it. Christ followers can usually break the power of a curse put on a person by naming or referring to the person who put it on and claiming God's power over it. Our words asserting our (and Jesus') authority over curses have the power to cancel them. People who come to Christ need to break the curses that have been put on them and also the curses they have put on others.

As for blessings, our words in the name of Jesus bring blessing, God's special favor, to the recipient. We have this authority by virtue of our relationship with Jesus. People often speak words lightly (like "Bless you" or "Be blessed") with little expectation of change. In many majority-world societies, God's blessing is recognized as actually carrying great power and is a significant practice for the local believers.

SOUL TIES

There are godly and ungodly soul ties where a person is spiritually bonded to another person. When they occur within a family, they can be a good thing, as with marriage or parenting. When they result in the domination of one person over another, as with extramarital sex, they are problematic.

Ungodly soul ties are empowered by Satan and involve the surrendering of free will. They need to be uncovered and canceled. They are usually easy to break in Jesus' name but can be troublesome if neglected.

---

1. I am familiar with some cases where formal curses need to be addressed by a group of believers, and with intentional prayer over a period of time.

SECTION FOUR

RECOMMENDED ACTIONS

Chapter 19

WHAT TO DO ABOUT FORBIDDEN CUSTOMS

IDENTIFYING WHICH CUSTOMS GOD is against is the easy part of our consideration. It is much more difficult to work out how to handle such customs in contemporary situations in a way that is loving and does not distract from the main messages of the gospel. We have learned, for example, that simply condemning customs such as polygamy and the drinking of traditional alcoholic beverages has in many places given Christianity a very disagreeable reputation. Unfortunately, such rules have kept many away from the kingdom because they were focused on secondary cultural changes supposedly required by God, rather than on the centrality of a relationship with Christ.

The Old Testament shows how strongly God is against such customs as the worship of other gods and divination. But the messages that make these points are directed to Jewish people—people whom God calls "his people." It is not surprising that God would want to warn his people concerning falling into idolatrous practices and attitudes. But is God's attitude on such matters the same toward those just coming out of former worldviews, who may still believe and practice some aspects of the lives they lived before embracing the good news? Can God be patient with former beliefs

SECTION FOUR: RECOMMENDED ACTIONS

and practices in the spiritual-power area, just as he is with non-ideal practices (e.g., polygamy, common law marriage) in other cultural areas?

The account of Naaman the Syrian whom God healed of leprosy through Elisha (2 Kgs 5) is possibly relevant here. As previously mentioned, Naaman was about to return to his country after being healed, and he requested

> two mule-loads of earth to take home with me, because from now on I will not offer sacrifices or burnt offerings to any god except the Lord. So I hope that the Lord will forgive me when I accompany my king to the temple of Rimmon, the god of Syria, and worship him. Surely the Lord will forgive me! (vv. 17–18)

The prophet Elisha responded, "Go in peace," presumably indicating that God would allow such a concession.

Given that God requires primary allegiance to himself (Exod 20:3), can we assume from the fact that Israel accepted the existence of many gods for some time, that God will allow this today? I believe we can. But the other gods and allegiances (e.g., family) have to be seen as secondary. Only the true God can be a believer's primary allegiance. It might not be too difficult for many people who believe in many gods to add Yahweh to their pantheon and to put him in first place. Perhaps even those who look to their ancestors would be willing to put God over them, as Israel did when they used the phrase "the God of Abraham, Isaac, and Jacob." The Israelites, like many animistic peoples, would gladly have pursued communication with Abraham, Isaac, and Jacob. But, to keep that from happening, they learned to focus on the God of these revered ancestors rather than on the ancestors themselves as entities with whom to interact.

As with all contexts where people are coming to faith in Christ, the crucial thing is the continued movement in the right direction. The point of a person's or group's choice to pledge allegiance to God through Christ needs to be followed by the process of greater and greater insight into and acceptance of God's ideals if the personal or cultural transformation is to continue in the right direction. And often this requires someone or something to keep encouraging the process and growth. If continued growth does not occur, the result will fall short of biblical faith.

Perhaps an illustration from language learning will help make this concept of "point plus process" clearer. In the first few weeks of a person's attempt to learn another language, they may not pronounce the words very well and will make numerous grammatical mistakes. But those helping people to learn will encourage them with compliments on how well they are doing, even though there are many mistakes. If, though, after five or ten years that person is making the same mistakes, the feedback will be different.

The language learner is encouraged in the early stages to be bold and to try to speak, even if they make many mistakes. But the person is expected to grow and improve in ability as time goes on. They need practice and the internal motivation to make themselves understood, as well as encouragement from others who may be helping in the language-learning process. So it is for new believers. They are expected to grow in their ability to practice their new faith but, like the language learner, will need the internal motivation and external encouragement to keep them growing.

As I have written in *Christianity in Culture*, being a Jesus follower is a spiritual direction. To follow Christ is to be one who is growing in the direction of greater Christ-likeness, not simply one who identifies as a Christian. It is not so much the position that one is in that makes one a believer, but the direction in which one is headed. Thus, the thief on the cross, in response to Jesus, turned and headed toward him. And he was saved. On the other hand, the Pharisees, who believed most of what Jesus taught and conscientiously practiced the commands of the Old Testament, were headed in the wrong direction because their motivation was not right. And they were lost.

I believe God is willing for those who have not known him to start with nothing more than a commitment to him, making him their primary allegiance. That commitment leads to understanding the changes that need to be made in a people's secondary allegiances and cultural practices. Such practices as communication

SECTION FOUR: RECOMMENDED ACTIONS

with ancestors, belief in reincarnation, seeking healing from shamans, divination in all of its many forms, and the like are to be turned away from as soon as possible, but not as preconditions for salvation. There is only one precondition: faith commitment to God through Jesus Christ.

Are the rules different for those who have been long-time recipients of God's revelation, such as the Hebrews, than for those who have not received such an advantage? They certainly are. Though the faith requirement—commitment to Jesus—is the same, the knowledge available to new believers makes a big difference in what is expected of them behaviorally. Though all are expected to change over time, the amount and kind of change will depend on where a person or group starts in that process. The thief on the cross started at a very long distance from ideal belief and behavior, with only one qualification for salvation: faith in Jesus. The believing Pharisees (and there were many) started their life of faith in Jesus with much of the expected behavior already habituated. And both the believing thief and the believing Pharisees were saved on the basis of their faith allegiance to Jesus—a faith allegiance that started them moving in a Christ-ward direction that meant salvation for them.

Chapter 20

DEVELOPING FUNCTIONAL SUBSTITUTES

ONCE FAITH IN JESUS is pledged, a lot of the ensuing growth may depend on whether or not other customs are developed to replace the customs that are judged to be inappropriate for believers. It is a sad fact of much missionary work that customs were condemned and, even more so, nothing was developed to take their place by serving the function previously served by the former custom. With regard to the power customs, this has usually resulted in people continuing to practice their former customs and allegiances, often in secret from missionaries and other outsiders. And in some places, such customs take place quite openly, even in the church buildings.

As mentioned earlier, they are practicing dual allegiance. They have embraced the new allegiance, often quite sincerely, but retained much of the old "just in case" the new doesn't cover everything.

The first and most important custom to be replaced is, of course, the primary faith commitment to gods, spirits, family, ideas, movements, or whatever else was the primary allegiance of the person or group. For it is this commitment that creates the dividing line between those who have decided to follow the good news, and those who have not yet decided to do so. There are,

SECTION FOUR: RECOMMENDED ACTIONS

however, other related customs to be replaced as well. The custom of seeking assistance from a shaman or occult practitioner is one. New believers need to learn how to appeal to the true God instead of to false gods for all their daily needs.

And this is where mission practice has often failed badly by not working with local peoples toward functional substitutes to replace former customs they deem spiritually harmful. A functional substitute is a custom or belief that serves the same function as the replaced custom did.

Often the habit of going to shamans has been condemned, but all that has been put in its place is a weak appeal to God in prayer or simply the use of a secular Western technique such as medicine or fertilizer. There is no ritual, authoritative use of the power of Christ to heal or bring fertility, or blessing of fields or animals. We should not ignore secular techniques, but we should also honor God by appealing to him first before using medical, agricultural, or other techniques that he has led people to discover.

For most of the traditional peoples of the world, healing, fertility, protection from misfortune, and the like are spiritual issues. They are not simply the human manipulation of physical substances, as seen in the West. Substitutes for certain customs should be conducted with primary concern for the spiritual nature of the problem and wrapped in meaningful ritual. Without substitutes, the people are left with a void in their experience that they will probably seek to fill by returning to their former practices.

A specific example of this problem would be the way funerals are conducted in areas where cross-cultural workers have lived. Traditional funerals usually involve a great deal of interaction with the spirit world. When such activity has been forbidden to new believers, with no practice that fills the void, they or their families typically satisfy themselves by doing much of that activity in secret.

How different things could be if traditional funerals were studied in order to identify cultural needs and develop, with local peoples, functional substitutes as needed, so that people's felt needs are met rather than ignored. The traditional concern over the involvement of the spirit world in death needs to be taken

Developing Functional Substitutes

seriously. Biblical functional substitutes must be culturally appropriate rituals that take care of the spiritual dimensions of life brought to the forefront by death. If this is not done, people will often expect and fear retribution from the spirits or gods that have not been properly satisfied.

When people believe that ancestors are involved in funeral exercises, their concerns should be taken seriously, and substitute understandings and rituals should be developed. As mentioned above, I believe it is possible to honor the ancestors in culturally appropriate ways, as long as God is recognized as primary. When ancestors are not given what the people believe is their due, and misfortune strikes, the people are all too ready to blame the lack of attention to ancestors' desires.

An example of working with the spiritual dimensions of new faith in culturally appropriate ways can be found in the Issan region of northeastern Thailand. Under the wise guidance of perceptive cross-cultural workers, the faith communities there have revised a custom used by the people to show their allegiance to spirits. The custom involves tying a string around the wrist as a symbol of several good things in an appropriate way. Originally the custom symbolizes dedication to spirits and a friendship commitment to other people. This custom has now been reworked by the believing community to symbolize new faith and love for one another. The traditional cultural felt need for such a ritual is thereby satisfied, though the meaning of the ritual has been reinterpreted for believers. Reforming a traditional ritual is reminiscent of the way God led Abraham to reform the ritual custom of circumcision and to reinterpret its meaning.

When it comes to divination, the problem of finding a functional substitute is made more difficult by the fact that God condemns the practice out of hand. We are forbidden to use any of the forms of divination to discern the future. However, God himself gives the spiritual gifts of prophecy, words of knowledge, and spiritual discernment (1 Cor 12:28–31). Believers can be taught to seek these gifts, to practice them, and to use them as God leads. And some will discover that God has gifted them in these areas. For the

SECTION FOUR: RECOMMENDED ACTIONS

sake of the Jesus-following community, they are able to function in many of the ways the diviners function, and with greater accuracy. Some may even find themselves regularly consulted, as diviners are, when something lost needs to be found or special advice from God is desired.

Dealing with magic and magical expectations can be another troublesome area. The essence of magic is to expect that if certain things are said or done, the desired result will be automatic. The great temptation is for people to try to control God through words or rituals that people regard as efficacious in getting him to do our will. The key change here is to help people recognize that the life of faith is to be a life of submission to God, not of controlling him. A part of this submission to him, however, involves the authority he gives us in ministry. And this, though not magic, can be even more powerful than magic. A part of the instruction people need on this subject is the fact that when people think they are able to control things through magic, what is really happening is that they are submitting unconsciously to satanic beings and power.

What I am suggesting, then, is that solid attention be given to developing biblical functional substitutes for the customs traditional people practice in the exercise of spiritual power. Many churches that have had missionary influence are, of course, already secularized in these matters—at least on the surface.

We ran into a situation on the island of Truk that is likely typical of many churches worldwide. My wife, while teaching on spiritual conflict to a group of about fifty pastors' wives, asked if there is any use of traditional power among their congregants. Without hesitation they said, "Yes, of course." In fact, they told my wife that they themselves often go to traditional spiritists when they feel they need a quick answer to their problems. "Our God is too slow," they said! No doubt the Western missionaries often responded to their problems with "let's pray about this," but did not follow through expecting God's immediate action.

I would suggest, then, that we also look in westernized churches for the ways in which spiritual power is sought and assist westernized Christians to meet their power needs in ways that

Developing Functional Substitutes

are more fitting with what we are instructed to do in the Bible. Many, of course, have been secularized and are not expecting God to work in power. They need to become more scriptural. Many others, however, have been meeting their power needs underground in traditional ways. These need help to discover that the powerful God of Scripture is still alive and doing powerful things in the present. Some groups set aside time in the worship service for believers to testify how God met their daily spiritual power needs. This helps all worshippers to recognize that God is alive and interested in providing the much-needed power for them.

And, if we desire to impact the world's power-oriented peoples whom Jesus loves, we need to be presenting the gospel with power. Jesus, working with a power-oriented people, used signs and wonders as a major part of his strategy. And he has passed this power on to us (John 14:12). Let's learn to do his work in his way—to move away from secular, powerless faith into a biblical faith which is always three dimensional (truth, allegiance, and power). Neglecting the power dimension of our faith has, I believe, made it more difficult for millions of people to follow Jesus. Let's not let that continue to happen.

Chapter 21

DIRECT BRIDGING FROM POWER TO POWER

WESTERN MODELS OF EVANGELISM, having largely ignored spiritual power issues, have tended to unwittingly recommend secularization as the antidote to traditional approaches to obtaining spiritual power. Western secular medicine and hospitals, for example, are offered as the answer to health problems. Secularizing schools are believed as the right way to deal with a Western perception of ignorance. There are secular agricultural techniques, secular approaches to church management and leadership, as well as insights into culture and communication that leave out the activity of the Holy Spirit.

With this approach, is it any wonder that churches started by Western missionaries around the world are deeply involved in secularizing their members? I believe it was Lesslie Newbigin who said that Christian missions have been the greatest secularizing force in all of history. Without intending it, then, the strategy has been to secularize in order to Christianize.

What this approach has produced is secular churches (like most of those in Western countries) that depend almost entirely on the power of secular techniques and structures to replace traditional methods of blessing, healing, teaching, and organizing.

Direct Bridging From Power to Power

There is, of course, a certain amount of power in these techniques. But they are dependent more on human and naturalistic powers than on spiritual power, even though they often replace what people have traditionally sought in spiritual ways. For example, for most of the traditional peoples of the world, healing, agriculture, and fertility have been spiritual matters, not secular ones. The West, however, has secularized each of these matters.

F. Douglas Pennoyer suggests that secularization can assist gospel outreach by breaking the domination of spiritual power in people's lives.[1] Though this may be true in some cases, I'm afraid secularization has for many peoples clouded rather than assisted much of what a scriptural approach to demonstrating the gospel should engender. For it has altered the process from what ought to have been a change from one spiritual power source to another (e.g., from satanic power to that of Jesus) into a change from spiritual answers to secular answers for problems that traditional peoples have always regarded as spiritual.

Simply moving from a forbidden power source to the true God as the source is, I believe, the shortest bridge for power-oriented people, since it involves little or no conversion from spiritual power to secular power. The conversion is, rather, from one power source (Satan) to another power source (God), as it was for Abraham. The cultural results of an approach that focuses on such change of power source are likely to be forms of faith in God through Jesus that look very similar to their original forms, but with a different power source. The Jesus-following practitioners would look very much like native shamans and other healers, but would work only in ways appropriate to biblical faith and only under the power of the true God. The places of worship and the ways in which worship and other rituals are conducted would look as much like what they knew formerly, as the places and rituals Abraham used to worship the true God looked like what he was familiar with.

As with Israel, the practices and personnel would undoubtedly change over time to be less like their former models. But they

---

1. Pennoyer, "In Dark Dungeons."

SECTION FOUR: RECOMMENDED ACTIONS

would have started at points familiar to the people rather than with foreign practices that give the impression that God's whole system has to be imported. And when prohibited practices in the spiritual power area (e.g., divination) are substituted for, let the substitution be a spiritual power substitution, not a secular one.

Chapter 22

KEY SPIRITUAL DYNAMICS IN INTERCULTURAL MINISTRY

As WE HAVE SEEN, there are quite a number of topics to recognize and address in ministry if we are to work as Jesus worked. Cross-cultural workers need to understand and be equipped to minister in spiritual power as well as with cultural and theological appropriateness. This means adding a strong component of spiritual dynamics to our missiological curriculum.

This attention to spiritual dynamics should address at least the following issues:

1. The authority given by Jesus. Jesus gave the Holy Spirit to his followers and with that gift gave them his own authority and power (Luke 9:1). We need to learn and teach that we have his power and how to use it in ministry to demonstrate God's love. Jesus said that whoever has faith in him will do the things he has been doing (John 14:12). Satan is afraid we will find this out and start doing the works of Jesus.[1]

2. The nature of the spiritual world around us. Because the spiritual world around us is invisible, we cannot see it like we see the physical world. However, based upon Scripture,

1. See Kraft, *I Give You Authority* and *Satan Fears* for more on our authority.

SECTION FOUR: RECOMMENDED ACTIONS

church history, and experience there is much we can know of the spiritual realm where both angels and demons dwell. We know that demons are opposed to God and can inhabit or attach themselves to humans. We know that angels are spirit beings who serve God and can help God's people in times of need. Of utmost importance, we need to remember that through Christ, God has entrusted us with power to have authority over evil spirits and set people free from demonic torment. Understanding and practicing this authority and imparting this knowledge to others is crucial.[2]

3. Demonization. Since many people in the world are carrying demons, we must learn and teach their existence and activities and how to deal with them. With Scripture as a starting point, we can learn and teach from books and articles written by those who have experience dealing with demons.

   For one thing, we need to learn that demons are a secondary problem. They can only be there if they are attached to something. It is, therefore, important to address the human issues through inner healing to weaken and force them away from a person.[3]

4. Dedications and soul ties. We need to learn and teach the conditions under which demons are passed on to the next generation of those dedicated to the spirits and how we can use Jesus' power to free people from such inheritance.

   Also, the dedication of lands, buildings, rituals, music, and other geographical and cultural phenomena can be broken and substituted with dedication to God. Especially in societies where people realize the power in words and practice dedications, we need to take dedication to Christ very seriously. We believe in the positive power of dedicating our children, new buildings, and perhaps other people and

---

2. See Kraft, *Confronting Powerless Christianity* for a brief introduction to the nature of evil spirits. See Kraft and DeBord, *Rules of Engagement* regarding principles and terms under which the spirit world operates.

3. For my take on this subject see Kraft, *Defeating Dark Angels*.

places. Soul ties occur when spiritual bonding takes place. Domination of one person over another results in ungodly soul ties. Satan's use of soul ties keeps people from being free.

5. Cursing and blessing. When we bless, God empowers our words and a spiritual transaction takes place.
6. Witchcraft and shamanism. These practices are prevalent in many parts of the world. There needs to be an understanding of how the local people relate to those they identify as occult practitioners, shamans, witches, or the like, and any resulting threats and fears. Again, the Holy-Spirit-power within the believer is our God-given weapon for resistance and liberation.
7. Gods, idols, and divination. As discussed above, cross-cultural workers need to be trained to recognize and deal with the spiritual beings and powers that compete with the true God. These spirits counterfeit the workings of God and keep people in captivity.
8. Who we are in Christ. I believe it frightens the devil and his followers that we might discover who we are and the authority and power God has given us. We need to know who we are in Christ and what difference this makes when we assert it in the spirit world. Among the publications on this subject is Neil Anderson's *Victory over the Darkness* and my *Satan Fears You'll Discover Your True Identity*. Additional writings are listed at the end of the book.

Teaching and practice on spiritual power has been neglected for too long. These are some of my suggested topics to address in ministry training to prepare candidates for dealing with the real world of spiritual power. There is much more to be said on each of these topics, but that needs to be developed by those teaching courses on these topics.

Those preparing to work cross-culturally should be well-versed in what to do about demons, dedicated places and things, occult practitioners, cursing, and whatever other expressions of spiritual power arise. They should recognize that God has

SECTION FOUR: RECOMMENDED ACTIONS

incredibly more power than Satan has and that clearing out the emotional and spiritual garbage to bring healing is the most important thing to do to defeat the enemy.

I have argued that the missiology that we have known has largely ignored spiritual-power issues even though the exercise of spiritual power was very much in evidence in Jesus' ministry. Jesus spent a lot of his time and energy healing and casting out demons.

Although issues of relationship and truth are rightly prominent in Jesus' ministry, I'm afraid the secular influence of Western Christianity has led us to ignore spiritual-power issues. We often rely on secular doctors and medicine for healing rather than turning to the healer who empowers the medicine and medical practitioners.

Western missionaries can introduce Western insight and technique into non-Western contexts but allow the impression that the power is in the techniques rather than in the spiritual reality behind the techniques. And Western missionaries tend to completely miss issues such as demonization that aren't reducible to naturalistic explanation.

Meanwhile, non-Western peoples often have greater insight into spiritual reality than Westerners. Though Western methods may better explain naturalistic phenomena, Western missiology often misses what is most important to non-Westerners. This book attempts to bring insight into the spiritual-power area that has been largely neglected in Western missiology. Cross-cultural ministry training should make this area a priority.

BIBLIOGRAPHY

Anderson, Neil. *Victory over the Darkness: Realize the Power of Your Identity in Christ*. Ventura, CA: Regal, 2000.
Beilby, James K., and Paul Rhodes Eddy. *Understanding Spiritual Warfare: Four Views*. Grand Rapids: Baker Academic, 2012.
Bishop, Brian. *Boundless: What Global Expressions of Faith Teach Us about Following Jesus*. Grand Rapids: Baker, 2015.
Dawkins, Robby. *Do Greater Things: Activating the Kingdom to Heal the Sick and Love the Lost*. Minneapolis: Chosen, 2018.
Dawson, John. *Taking Our Cities for God*. Lake Mary, FL: Creation House, 1989.
Engelsviken, Tormod. "Spiritual Conflict: A Challenge for the Church in the West with a View to the Future." In *Paradigm Shifts in Christian Witness*, edited by Charles Van Engen et al., 116–25. Maryknoll, NY: Orbis Books, 2008.
Hiebert, Paul. "The Flaw of the Excluded Middle." *Missiology* 10 (1982) 35–47.
Hiebert, Paul, et al. *Understanding Folk Religion: A Christian Response to Popular Beliefs and Practices*. Grand Rapids: Baker, 2000.
Keener, Craig. *Miracles: The Credibility of the New Testament Accounts*. 2 vols. Grand Rapids: Baker Academic, 2011.
———. *Miracles Today: The Supernatural Work of God in the Modern World*. Grand Rapids: Baker Academic, 2021.
Kraft, Charles H. "Christian Animism or God-Given Authority?" In *Spiritual Power and Missions*, edited by Edward Rommen, 88–136. Pasadena: William Carey Library, 1995.
———. *Christianity in Culture: A Study in Dynamic Biblical Theologizing in Cross-Cultural Perspective*. Rev. 25th anniversary ed. Maryknoll, NY: Orbis, 2005.
———. *Confronting Powerless Christianity*. Grand Rapids: Baker, 2002.
———. *Defeating Dark Angels*. Rev. ed. Ventura, CA: Regal, 2011.
———. *I Give You Authority: Practicing the Authority Jesus Gave Us*. Grand Rapids: Chosen, 1997.
———. *Satan Fears You'll Discover Your True Identity*. Grand Rapids: Chosen/Baker, 2019.

Bibliography

———. "What Kind of Encounters Do We Need in Our Witness?" In *Evangelical Missions Quarterly* 27 (1991) 258–65.
Kraft, Charles H., ed. *Behind Enemy Lines: An Advanced Guide to Spiritual Warfare*. Ann Arbor: Servant, 1994. Reprint, Pasadena: Wipf & Stock, 2000.
Kraft, Charles H., and David DeBord. *The Rules of Engagement*. Eugene, OR: Wipf & Stock, 2000.
Lewis, C. S. *The Screwtape Letters*. London: Geoffrey Bles, 1942.
MacNutt, Francis. *Healing*. Rev ed. Notre Dame, IN: Ave Maria, 1999.
Muller, Ann. *Two Hands: A Guide for Inner Healing Prayer*. San Diego: Access, 2020.
Pennoyer, F. Douglas. "In Dark Dungeons of Collective Captivity." In *Wrestling with Dark Angels*, edited by Peter Wagner and Douglas Pennoyer, 250–79. Ventura, CA: Regal, 1990.
Priest, Robert J., et al. "Missiological Syncretism: The New Animistic Paradigm." In *Spiritual Power and Missions*, edited by Edward Rommen, 9–47. Pasadena: William Carey Library, 1995.
Silvoso, Edgardo. "Prayer Power in Argentina." In *Engaging the Enemy: How to Fight and Defeat Territorial Spirits*, edited by C. Peter Wagner, 109–15. Ventura, CA: Regal, 1991.
Thompson, Jon. *Deliverance: A Journey Toward the Unexpected*. Ontario, Canada: Sanctus Church, 2021.
Travis, John, and Anna Travis. "Deep-Level Healing Prayer in Cross-Cultural Ministry: Models, Examples, and Lessons." In *Paradigm Shifts in Christian Witness*, edited by Charles Van Engen et al., 106–15. Maryknoll, NY: Orbis, 2008.
Vaughan, Joy L. *Phenomenal Phenomena: Biblical and Multicultural Accounts of Spirits and Exorcism*. Waco: Baylor University Press, 2023.
Wagner, C. Peter. "Missiology and Spiritual Power." In *Paradigm Shifts in Christian Witness*, edited by Charles Van Engen et al., 91–97. Maryknoll, NY: Orbis, 2008.
Wagner, C. Peter, ed. *Breaking Strongholds in Your City*. Ventura, CA: Regal, 1993.
———. *Engaging the Enemy: How to Fight and Defeat Territorial Spirits*. Ventura, CA: Regal, 1991.
Wagner, C. Peter, and Douglas Pennoyer, eds. *Wrestling with Dark Angels: Toward a Deeper Understanding of the Supernatural Forces in Spiritual Warfare*. Ventura, CA: Regal, 1990.
Wagner, C. Peter, and Rebecca Greenwood. "The Strategic-Level Deliverance Model." In *Understanding Spiritual Warfare: Four Views*, edited by James K. Beilby and Paul Rhodes Eddy, 173–98. Grand Rapids: Baker Academic, 2012.
Wimber, John. *Power Evangelism*. 1986. Rev. ed. San Francisco: Harper & Row, 1992.
———. *Power Healing*. San Francisco: Harper & Row, 1987.

Bibliography

Woodbury, J. Dudley. "Power and Blessing: Keys for Relevance to a Religion as Lived." In *Paradigm Shifts in Christian Witness*, edited by Charles Van Engen et al, 98–105. Maryknoll, NY: Orbis, 2008.

———. "The Relevance of Power Ministries for Folk Muslims." In *Wrestling with Dark Angels: Toward a Deeper Understanding of the Supernatural Forces in Spiritual Warfare*, edited by Peter Wagner and Douglas Pennoyer, 313–31. Ventura, CA: Regal, 1990.

BOOKS ON SPIRITUAL POWER BY CHARLES H. KRAFT

Appropriate Christianity. Pasadena, CA: William Carey Library, 2005

Behind Enemy Lines: An Advanced Guide to Spiritual Warfare. Ann Arbor, MI: Servant, 1994

Confronting Powerless Christianity. Grand Rapids, MI: Baker, 2002

Dealing with Demons. Eugene, OR: Wipf & Stock, 2017

Deep Wounds, Deep Healing. 1993. Rev. ed. Ventura, CA: Regal, 2010

Defeating Dark Angels. 1992. Rev. ed. Ventura, CA: Regal, 2011

The Evangelical's Guide to Spiritual Warfare. Grand Rapids, MI: Baker, 2015

I Give You Authority: Practicing the Authority Jesus Gave Us. Grand Rapids, MI: Chosen, 1997

Power Encounter in Spiritual Warfare. Eugene, OR: Wipf & Stock, 2017

The Rules of Engagement, with David M. DeBord. Eugene, OR: Wipf & Stock, 2000

Satan Fears You'll Discover Your True Identity. Grand Rapids, MI: Chosen, 2019

Two Hours to Freedom: A Simple and Effective Model for Healing and Deliverance. Grand Rapids, MI: Chosen, 2010

www.ingramcontent.com/pod-product-compliance
Lightning Source LLC
Chambersburg PA
CBHW072200160426
43197CB00012B/2466